Facing the Dark Side of *Genesis*

Facing the Dark Side of *Genesis*

A New Understanding of Ourselves

Robert E. Joyce

LifeCom

Published by
LifeCom
St. Cloud, Minnesota, USA

© 2008   Robert E. Joyce
All rights reserved

ISBN   978-0-615-25187-5

No part of this book may be used or reproduced in any manner whatsoever without written permission. No part of this book may be stored in a retrieval system or transmitted in any form or by any means including electronic, electrostatic, magnetic tape, mechanical, photocopying, recording or otherwise without the prior permission of the publisher.

For information, address *LifeCom*, Box 1832, St. Cloud, MN 56302

Contents

Preface

One	The Dark Side of *Genesis*	1
Two	Why Revisit the Dawn of Creation?	5
Three	The *Genesis* Gap	9
Four	Originative Sin	11
Five	Theology of the Person's Being	19
Six	Toward an Ontology of Creation	25
Seven	From Forming and Being Formed to Giving and Receiving	29
Eight	Two Creations: Originative and Redemptive	37
Nine	True Receiving Is Pure Activity	41
Ten	The Redemptive Creation	47
Eleven	Consequences for Our Lives of Faith	51
Twelve	The Light on *Genesis*	63
Glossary		69

Preface

This book comes from contemplating the structure of reality that includes our spiritually unconscious selves.

In the 20th Century, we became aware of the psychological unconscious and its imperious effects on human growth and development. But we are still not seriously considering a part of ourselves that is unconscious *spiritually*. While we meditate upon the *Genesis* account of origins and the immediate darkness that it portrays, we are repressing the originative structure of our being.

In assessing our condition, I want to acknowledge preceding thinkers and movements of thought. Deeply appreciated, for instance, are insights in psychoanalytic development. But especially valuable is the perennial wisdom of Plato, Aristotle, St. Thomas Aquinas, and John Paul II.

Aristotle discovered metaphysics. This science of being as being begins only after the attainment of a basic knowledge of the philosophy of nature. St. Thomas was preeminently a theologian who utilized the philosophy of Aristotle, especially metaphysics, in his comprehensive Christian synthesis. John Paul II was an anthropological theologian and a phenomenological philosopher who developed his inspiring theology of the body and other perspectives somewhat independently of Thomistic concepts, yet thoroughly rooted in the tradition. The Fathers of the Church, East and West, provided the bedrock of this tradition of Faith and reason.

The ensuing reflections are indebted particularly to some of the perspectives of Plato, Aristotle, Aquinas, and others, but are not fixed on them. My effort here is a brief ontology of *Genesis*.

Ontology begins with our immediate intellectual *and volitional* union with the being that we know. Our immediate presence to this being might be intense or weak. But, in this way of knowing, every being—person or non-person—is esteemed as being radically other than nothing and as a gift to be received.

Ontological knowledge is not the same as metaphysics. It precedes our concepts, inductions, and deductions; and it *causes* all of them.

This causal knowing is essentially independent of our senses, and is active *through* our senses, and *beyond* our senses—all at once. Our sense perceptions, concepts, and the rest are constituted within our *ontological power* for knowing being.

Because animals do not have the ability to know *being*, they cannot know that they are beings—other than nothing. If they could know in this way, they could wonder why they exist. They could even distinguish between their *ex-(s)istence* and their *being*, and could become ontological philosophers.

The content of Faith, of what is given in Revelation, is not the same as theology, the systematic renderings of its meaning.

While challenging some traditional theological assumptions, the changed theistic worldview in this book should threaten no one who is Christian. Everything offered is plausible within the guidelines of divine Revelation—and specifically *possible* within the teaching authority of the Roman Catholic Church, to which I am committed for life.

The reader is encouraged to be open to a new framework for thoughts about reality. One should not read comments and claims as rigidly attached to time-worn meanings for everyday terms. The worldview being presented challenges some of those meanings, at least in part. When the origins of the cosmos and of humanity are at issue, two-dimensional communication will not do. In this essay, then, a third dimension is introduced, particularly pertaining to the spiritual unconscious.

A **Glossary** of important terms provides aid to the reader in assimilating the newer meanings. The Glossary is structured topically and can be read as a whole. Or terms can be consulted briefly, as they are encountered in the main body of the book.

One

The Dark Side of *Genesis*

The Book of Genesis begins with a mysterious void and darkness (*Genesis* 1:2). Next comes God's creation of light (*Genesis* 1:3). Since the supreme Being is infinitely perfect, without any darkness at all, why was there a void and darkness within God's creation *before* light appeared? Where did that darkness come from?

The void is significant because it means an absence of something that is supposed to *be* there. Darkness, too, indicates a lack: the absence of light. A void or darkness is not the same as *nothing*, since nothing does not signify the absence of something.

So, what is this primal emptiness? Whatever it is, in accord with *Genesis*, it would have to be the imperfect condition from which the rest of cosmic creation came forth.

We can begin to realize then that *Genesis* is not a foundational explanation of creation as such. One obvious reason is that there is no reference to the creation of the angels.

Of all creatures, these simply spiritual beings are most like God. They are finite persons glorifying infinite Persons. Their presence is mentioned frequently in Sacred

Facing the Dark Side of Genesis

Scripture. They even appear in *Genesis*. But, in the story of origins, God's creation of them is not explicitly recognized.[1]

The account in *Genesis* 1 tells *explicitly* only about the other kind of finite persons, the human ones. They first appear at the end of the initial description of cosmic creation. Yet, these persons are cited in the *Psalms* as "a little less than the angels."[2]

Why is there such a huge chasm of being between the creations of the two kinds of finite persons, angelic and human? Angels had to have been created instantly with no passive matter involved—neither time nor space. Humans,

---

[1] St. Augustine saw the creation of angels as symbolized by the references to the heavens and to the light. This anagogical (mystical, allegorical) rendition might seem to edify angels who are 'learning about creation,' as Augustine interpreted it, but it does not do much to account for the world as it can be viewed by humans on earth.

Rather, the creation accounts in *Genesis* should be taken to refer principally and overwhelmingly to the creation of the cosmic world, with "the heavens" indicating the panoply of stars and planets in the sky. The text obviously refers to such matters, even as it offers much additional intelligibility that can be gleaned by meditative reading.

Moreover, figurative and literal senses can be adjudicated, especially under the integrative light of an ontological understanding that mediates between various kinds of interpretation. When all is said and done, the analogical meanings (figurative, symbolic, allegorical, anagogical) can be finally "read," as Augustine might say, by the angels and the saints. For now, something less would seem to be more important.

[2] Lack of clarity respecting the likeness and difference between angels and humans is curiously shown in the recent translations of *Psalms* 8:6 about God creating humankind "a little less than the angels." Some of the recent English editions have rendered the text by expressions such as "a little less than God," or "a little less than gods."

Important ontological work is needed to challenge the suggestion that any created person is to be "compared" to God, and to support the traditional understanding of the relationship between created persons: angelic and human. We are *supremely related to* God and *like* God, but we are in nowise gods, nor comparable to God. The uses of words, such as *elohim* and *angelos*, need sound ontological interpretation.

The Dark Side of Genesis

however, are presented as created at the culmination of a process. The whole of the cosmos did not originate instantly, but part by part, so to speak—whether the process lasted days or eons.[3]

Both angels and humans are persons—essentially spiritual. Were not such beings created together out of nothing? Why was the creation of the non-angelic persons preceded by a void and darkness—gross imperfections?

Did something happen in the domain of created *persons*—some kind of a big issue—that caused a void and darkness in it? Could such an "absence of something," explain the momentous gap in the community of created persons?

---

[3] St. Augustine speculated about the whole cosmos as being created all at once, in one "day," with the gradual unfolding of eventual existence that was only potential at first. But the issue here is the creation of perfect actuality, not passive potentiality. By the creating act of the infinitely perfect, only the finitely perfect can result, including perfect *freedom*.

Augustine's notion of a package of powers for instantly created reality meant that most cosmic being was destined to unfold gradually. So, even he saw original creation as involving process, necessarily signifying some lack of perfection from the start.

Despite his special anagogical intuition about God and creation, Augustine, too, seems to miss the full force of creation *ex nihilo* (*out of nothing*).

On the one hand, such creation could *only* be of *perfect* persons, effected by the infinitely perfect act of God. These created persons—both angelic and human—are not "gifted" originatively with *any* passive potency or with processes, in which the passively potential becomes actualized.

On the other hand, every *subpersonal* being is *essentially imperfect*. Each had to have been created out of some kind of a *void*—not out of "nothing." A "void" is an emptiness within something, even within a fullness. What is the something or the fullness with respect to this void?

Two

Why Revisit the Dawn of Creation?

If God did not reveal something, then it is obviously not necessary for our salvation. Is there any need, then, for a reconsideration of creation?

Yes. Scriptural Revelation comes both in the words and between the lines. Future developments of meaning can raise to awareness what is originally only implied. For instance, the scientific progress of recent centuries has seriously challenged exclusively literal interpretations of *Genesis*. As a result, the faith of multitudes has been shaken.

So, we now realize better our need for more than the words of *Genesis*. We look more seriously for what these words really mean. Traditional Biblical scholarship is immensely helpful, though easily neglected. Besides, it too needs deeper ontological foundations.

Moreover, at the turn of the 21st century, New Age worldviews are thriving. In many peoples, theism is giving way to various forms of an almost pandemic pantheism. Transcendent meaning concerning creation *ex nihilo* (out of nothing) and sin is rapidly losing ground.

Facing the Dark Side of Genesis

The challenge is profound. No longer can we continue to offer inadequate explanations for evil, such as the one about God drawing good out of evil.[4] In a post-holocaust world, Faith needs much deeper reasoning to support it.

Fides (faith) requires ever more meaningful levels of *ratio* (reason).[5] Contemporary authors have been freely presenting their challenges to religious belief. Threatening the Judeo-Christian worldview are a train of popular books, including *Night* by Eli Wiesel, *When Bad Things Happen to Good People* by Harold Kushner, *A History of God* by Karen Armstrong, *How to Know God* and *The Third Jesus* by Deepak Chopra, and many others. Theists are put on notice that the traditional meanings for God, for creation, and for evil must truly deepen lest millions more slip away.[6]

---

[4] Out of evil as evil, only evil can be drawn. God is not a magician. God draws good out of good, despite even massive degrees of evil being involved. Only goodness has potential for greater good. Evil as evil has no potential for good.

The bigger questions include how evil ever originated from a totally good creation and how God could allow innocent persons to suffer at the hands of monstrous evil, material and spiritual.

[5] In the Encyclical, *Fides et Ratio*, Pope John Paul II called emphatically for philosophers to bring metaphysics to bear on matters of faith. The need is incomparable considering the maelstrom of currents in theology and philosophy today.

[6] Generally, Jewish and Christian theologians have avoided facing squarely the "dark side of *Genesis*." From commentaries on the *Book of Job* to contemporary guidance, spiritual writers offer particularly good insights on how to suffer well, but slide away from saying *why* even the most innocent of us must suffer. This unconscious *denial* of personal responsibility for the origin of evil is taken to an extreme in a strain of contemporary Jewish thought by the "theology of protest," according to which the holocaust revealed God's insufficient caring for His people. Followers of David Blumenthal even enjoin God to "repent to us" for His failure. Cf. David Blumenthal, *Facing the Abusing God: A Theology of Protest* (Louisville, Ky.: Westminster John Knox Press, 1993).

Why Revisit the Dawn of Creation?

For the sake of strengthening our faith in the divine revelation of *Genesis*, we need to receive and discern the very meaning of *being* and of *being-at-all*. A serious and substantially richer ontology of creation would help us to develop our traditional beliefs, and not to slip away from them.

Three

The *Genesis* Gap

We know by faith that we are destined for the community of all persons in the ecstatically joyful presence of God: Father, Word, Spirit, good angels, and saints. Why then are we humans here at all, rather than already there? Why are we all "spaced out" and "doing time"?

Since God is infinite, and not arbitrary, there must be a supremely good reason why we now find ourselves in a profoundly ambivalent world that is both magnificent and explosive—both beautiful and dangerous—with rainbows, sunsets, and clear mountain streams as well as disease, darkness, and death. Even before the Fall in Eden, Adam and Eve were threatened by an "in your face" object (an ambivalent tree) that combined good with evil, and by the presence of a serpentinian tempter.

Also, in faith and reason, we know our souls were created directly by God "out of nothing," even as were the angels. But then the vast abyss between ourselves and the angels seems to force us to believe that *human* personhood is somehow a put-together thing, like an artifact. Our soul and body are often regarded as components of our being that come together from two different directions, rather than being a soul that expresses itself bodily within itself.

Facing the Dark Side of Genesis

The apparently independent origins of body and soul beg for better explanation. Does God wait upon sperm and ovum and then interact with them by zapping the zygote with a spiritual soul? In creating human persons, is God at the mercy of teenagers in the back seat of a car and beholden to adulterers and fornicators of all kinds? God seems to be regarded in a behavioristic way, with the creature providing the stimulus and the Creator yielding the response. The implied meaning makes the creation of human persons seem rather like an expediential rationalization—a *creatio ex machina*.

Our personal creation *ex nihilo* (out of nothing) has been presented as dependent on the radical contingencies of nature's physical processes. But if that is so, then the human person, as a spiritual soul "infused into" a matter that is somewhat independently disposed, is similar to an unnatural, fictional composite, like a centaur or mermaid.

Instead, we need to realize that every person's body—despite appearances—comes *not* from the impersonal forces of Nature, but from within his or her own being. The human body is the sacramentive expression of the person's *being*—a being that is groping for redemption and salvation.

Four

Originative Sin

Our creation story in *Genesis* starts with a void and darkness. That kind of beginning must be significant. *Sin* had entered somehow. We are called to realize a deeper dimension to the *original sin* of our first parents.

Adam and Eve, for instance, were created out of dust, that is, from some prior condition of lowly significance. Despite the disparity of sources, we can ask, "Is the dust of their origin related to the darkness and the void, so vividly expressed earlier?"

And is there an even prior effect-to-cause connection. Is the void, or the dust itself, caused by a pre-cosmic fall from spiritual light into the darkness, out of which the cosmos began to emerge? If so, what could that cause be?

At the *non-durational* moment or instant of creation *ex nihilo*—not reported in *Genesis* directly—God said, "Be." All created beings—directly out of nothing—were perfect finite persons.[7] They were not merely "good" or "very

---

[7] God must have said not only "Be," but "Be with Us" in the communion of persons. Creation *ex nihilo* is essentially an interpersonal act *of* Persons *for* persons. In that act, God necessarily and immediately intends that the *being* of each created person responds as a person—immediately, without being impeded by space and time or by anything else.

good." All were *perfect*. They were created by *God* who is both unlimitedly good and unlimitedly powerful. Not merely one or the other. The infinite Creator *could* not create anything originatively or *out of nothing* that was even slightly imperfect (and still be God). We must face not only the darkness of origins, but the light. The *light* we must face is the perfect being that we are immediately and the infinitely perfect Creator that God is.

All of these creatures were persons and persons only—angelic and human.[8] There could be *no* subpersonal, intrinsically imperfect beings, such as atoms, minerals, plants, and animals. These came later, as the result of something imperfect that could not have originated solely and directly from God.

As God said, "Be," all created beings (persons only) were completely free to say *yes*, immediately and fully. Due to their natural simplicity of being, angels could say either *yes* or *no*. Human beings, perfect yet more complex by nature, could say *yes, no,* or *maybe.* Every created person knew God directly and immediately—not in glory, but in the personal infinity of Being.

Why would *any* person say *no* or even *maybe*? Faced with the opportunity to receive their being as gifted and as finite, many persons determined themselves to desire an infinite being or personhood—the kind of being of God, the Gifter. In effect, they either rebelled or were indecisive. They either willed to be infinite along with

---

[8] Human persons were perfect, spiritually and materially—and not (yet) expressed in space and time. Their kind of perfection was more complex ontologically than that of angels. Chapter Five, "Theology of the Person's Being," offers a definition of *originative* matter as *purely active receptivity* within the human essence—not the passive, opaque kind we know now. Chapter Nine delineates the difference in essence between angels and humans.

Originative Sin

God, whom they knew was gifting them with being, or they were not sure about willing to be "merely" finite.

Most of the angels said an immediate *yes* to their perfect finite being. The others said an immediate *no*.

Human persons, however, were gifted with a more complex kind of *perfect* personhood. Some of them, also, might have said an immediate *yes* or *no*. Still others of their kind, such as we—apparently very many—hesitated by saying *maybe*: a mix of *yes* and *no*. In other words, as it were, "Let me think about it." So, we were immediately gifted with "space and time" to do so.

All of the immediate *yes*-sayers, by virtue of their fullness of good will, entered into the glory of God in supreme joy immediately and forever. Multitudes of angels did. Perhaps a few or many human persons did likewise. So precarious and ego-centric is our present plight, we do not even think about the possibility that some of our kind said immediately and fully *yes*.

Besides the *freedom* to say fully *yes*, all created persons—as finite beings—were *able* to respond with less than *yes*. Many angels, of whom Lucifer was most prominent, said fully *no*. Perhaps many or a few originative humans did likewise. All of these *fully-no-*sayers thereby frustrated immediately the gift of their being forever. They were unredeemable because their own will was completely negative—closing off even a partial *yes* with which God could have willed to redeem them.

By contrast, we humans who are, as a result of our originatively imperfect self-determination, living on the planet earth in the spatiotemporal cosmos must have said *maybe*—partly *yes* and partly *no*. We were freely and immediately *diffident* about being finite.

Facing the Dark Side of *Genesis*

Some of us may have said more *yes* than *no*; others, more *no* than *yes*. There must have been many degrees of *maybe*-saying. From our cast-out condition now, it would be in vain to speculate who said what degree of *maybe* at that primal point.[9]

The resulting poverty in our individual beings would seem to be immense: spiritually, intellectually, mentally, emotionally, physically, *et al.* We can know *that* it is so and something of its nature, without knowing anything about individuals. Many who are wealthy materially are in poverty spiritually. Others, who are in poverty materially, can be also in poverty mentally and spiritually. *Lazarus* and *Dives* are living together in the same world. But only by their fruits will we know them.

In any case, we *maybe*-sayers crashed, and each one of us fell into massive passivity, created by the *no* in our *maybe*. Even those saying the slightest *no* would have gone into a pre-cosmic ontological coma: into the darkness

---

[9] Our jaded vision is inclined to reduce ontological and theological issues to a cosmotheological perspective. We are cosmolocked. Our intellects are ordered to the quiddity (whatness) of sensible things.

But not by God. By us and our originative sin. And we are strongly inclined to be fixated there, even when contemplating the Trinity, creation, *et al*.

Traditionalists have often given undue devotion to the scholastic dictum that "nothing is in the intellect except what was somehow first in the senses." But none of this "transition" from senses to intellect could occur without the intellect itself being its adequate cause—not merely as a function of *agent* intellect "servicing the senses," but as a fully *knowing* agent power.

Originative sin has made us inclined to deny our free and simultaneous access to the spiritual and ontological—independent of the sensory intrinsically *and* extrinsically. But, for conscious everyday thoughts in this world, we are *also*, of course, dependent on our senses and their cooperative relation to our intellect and will. This world of human intellection is paradoxical in relation to sensory knowing—*both* dependent extrinsically on the senses *and* independent of *any* physical sensory input.

Originative Sin

of a void. So offensive would such a sin be to our own being's gift from *unlimited* goodness, love, and intimacy.

The hesitation in our *yes*-saying caused the *need* for the world in which we now live—the backwaters of creation. God responded to the *yes* in our *maybe* by the unconditional and infinitely loving activity of creating for our limping existence a life-line: this life in space and time. Such derivative creation was drawn out of something (*ex aliquo*): out of our self-fragmented being. We were able thus to be-come: to be able to come back from our originative crash, along with Adam and Eve, our first parents in this present world of recuperation and recovery.

We might expect that the merely *partial yes,* coming from our perfect being with perfect freedom, would have emitted an ontological explosion that became the passive-reactive (*no-yes*) energy, out of which God began to form the cosmos. Space and time were created to serve the recovery process that, for each person would go, hopefully, from *no-yes* at creation *ex nihilo* to a fullness of *yes* before or at death. In other words, our *no-yes* would become resolved into either a *yes* or a *no* forever.

We need to realign our thinking about origins. The *originative* sin of Adam and Eve was committed along with us, at the moment that, with them and all other persons, we were created together out of nothing, perfectly and immediately. Then, in the whole economy of redemption, our primal parents were the first of us to be formed from the 'dust of the earth' and from their own share in self-caused passivity. We were given a quasi-placental life in space and time.

Adam and Eve happened to be those persons whom God placed first in the line of recovery through existence in the cosmic (redemptive) creation. Thanks to their life in Eden,

Facing the Dark Side of *Genesis*

they were put on the way to their actual redemption and possible salvation. In *Genesis*, God pronounced all of the creatures of the cosmos *good*. The whole of the redemptive creation was indeed *very good*.

All *maybe*-sayers were gifted with redemption and the opportunity for salvation. We humans who hesitated to be, and to be who we were gifted to be, were graced by God's unconditional, unlimitedly responsive (not reactive) love.

After their remedial creation in the Garden, the first couple ate the forbidden fruit. The deed was a foregone conclusion. God had said to Adam, "The day you eat of it, you shall die the death." Allowing the direct disobedience was God's way of awakening them to how weak they had made themselves by originatively failing to receive fully the *gift* of their *being*.

The sin of Eden was a "wake up call" regarding their underlying self-induced imperfection of *be*-ing.[10] They had done what we all did. They had caused this tragic flaw originatively. But, with us all, they immediately repressed it, spiritually and severely, into part of their very ontological structure. They and we caused the whole of the unconscious, into which the sin was thrust. Then, on being given a quasi-placental lifeline that was created *ex aliquo* (out of the dust of the earth), their ensuing disobedience to God's explicit command in the Garden alerted them and brought exposure to their own nakedness of *being*.

At the moment of creation *ex nihilo*, God had created them—and all of us humans—as whole free beings, individually and communally. This creation of all

---

[10] The word *being* is hyphenated to indicate that it is an act that we *do*, the root act of all others, such as breath-ing, think-ing, lov-ing. Our act of *be*-ing is not some abstract principle, but a dynamic act gifted by God for us to *do*, necessarily: the supreme active potency that we *are* originatively.

Originative Sin

persons—finitely perfect in all respects, including the perfect freedom to love God totally—is not the creation written about explicitly in *Genesis*. This one (*ex nihilo*) was primordial: all light, resulting in perfect (finite) persons. A perfect creation.

The perfect wholeness of human persons must have included a kind of "pre-physical" matter or principle of purely active receptivity. In anyone who willfully hesitated to be the person they were gifted to be, this active potency to receive became passivized, spatial and temporal, that is, bodied. This physicalization (good partly: as redemptive) was caused by our imperfect act of *be*-ing—made so by exercising somewhat weakly the perfect gift of God (our power to receive *being* fully). The freedom-power was *perfect*. The *act*, done with this perfect freedom, was not.[11]

In our be-ing, we were thereby giftedly perfect, but receivedly imperfect. There was no interval between God's act of creating and our act of receiving the gift. By our gifted be-ing, we acted somewhat counter to that being. All was effected *freely at once*.

We freely fragmented ourselves by our *maybe*: both imploding and exploding our own beings. The crash was in the structure of our being; it was ontological, not cosmological. The cosmos is *part* of the recovery.

Only we created persons who said *maybe* would need redemption—a booster creation, so to speak. This

---

[11] The unique person did the act, not the God-gifted perfect power. Acts are not done by powers, but by persons, who act responsibly or irresponsibly in exercising their powers. As Thomas Aquinas noted for us, *hic homo intellegit,* this whole singular person understands. The intellect does not, but affords the *power* for the act of understanding that is the personal agent's *doing*. Similarly, we could say, *hic homo amat,* this whole person loves. The will does not. The *lover* does.

Facing the Dark Side of *Genesis*

derivative creation came not *ex nihilo*, but *ex aliquo* (out of something, namely, the condition of self-decimation or void that our originative personal sin had caused). Out of a chaos God created the cosmos.

In this new order of being—the order of *becoming* (*being* trying to come back fully to itself)—it seems that our bodies come directly from nature, rather than directly from God. They come ultimately from God, of course, but our bodies are really a kind of receptivity: a weakened receptivity, conditioned by our having hesitated with Eve and Adam in a non-durational, pristine order of immediately gifted, perfect being.

Our bodily, passive, spatiotemporal existence, then, is *both* defective *and* good. It is defective that we had to have such a "temporal and spatial extension" of our being and our freedom. But it is also good that we *could* have it, that we were redeemable because we did not say simply *no* to being and to being-with God. In our *maybe*—our first, signature act of freedom—there is a greatness of *yes*, subtly blended with the *no*.[12]

---

[12] Many Christians believe in the efficacy of purgation after death for those whose commitment of mind and heart is adequate, but falls short of full, personal restoration during the present life. We can truly claim Jesus as our Savior and yet reveal, in our actions and attitudes, some measure of *imperfection of sincerity*. Our cleansing must be perfect before it is possible to be as spiritually pure as we were gifted to be in originative creation and before we can possibly be present to the full glory of God.

Five

Theology of the Person's Being

In our own times, we have benefited from a theory developed by Pope John Paul II. It is called a "theology of the body"—the human body revealing a likeness to God. But we have hardly begun to see that, in the *first* beginning, our personal matter was not at all passive and physical. Matter was purely (immediately and perfectly) active and recep*tive* of our own *being.*

In our supreme beginning, God must have created both form and matter, in the divine likeness, as purely active dimensions of our essence: correlative capacities to give (form) and to receive (matter). *Active* giving and *active* receiving are the essence of personhood *as gifted originatively.*

In this primal beginning, we were *able* to receive God, self, and others, immediately, perfectly, and permanently. But we did not. As it is, then, we are passive and spatiotemporal because, at the moment of the creation, we poorly acted with this gifted structure of prototypical freedom. Not a deliberative kind of freedom as we have now, this freedom was a freedom of being—of who we are or will to be.[13]

Yet we fail to acknowledge our *originative* sin. So, for instance, we proceed to treat conception as the beginning of our being, rather than as the beginning of our functional be-coming (being coming back from our ontological collapse) through the world of space and time.[14]

Besides a "theology of the body," we need an "ontological theology of the person's being." The *whole being* would be understood as gifted immediately and solely by God and *received immediately by self*—whether totally, partially, or not at all.

---

[13] Such gifted freedom was all grace. We were created in grace, in God's love. This grace was not nature as we know it in this fallen life, but a nature able to form a complete *union* (not an identity) with God's *infinite* nature. This originative freedom-nature was our supernature, that is, super or above the nature with which we now operate, for the most part: one that is severely flawed by ourselves and in need of the grace of God that could have been ours from the moment of creation *ex nihilo*, if we had not demurred.

Grace can mean various things: the very life of God, the immediate presence of God, communion with the divine, and so forth. Our present fractual freedom—fractured actual freedom—depends for its effectiveness on our choosing from alternatives, some of which choices can indicate our strength of will to *be-with* God as God ever wills for us. By such fallen, but good-hearted choosing, we can reveal our openness to divine life. We can will to let God save and restore us to what God 'had' prepared for those who love Him—and still *has* prepared for those who repent sincerely. But we must *will* to help God save us—*ex aliquo*, out of something crashed, void, and dark.

[14] Before conception, the whole being of the fallen human person would have been, as it were, ontologically comatose (a hypersomnolent be-ing), resulting from the originative, personal sin. We self-crashed human beings would have been participating in passive matter lethargically, as it were, but not with any formal awareness. Our *formal* becoming and participation in space and time must have begun at the moment of conception—God's creation of us *ex aliquo* (out of *something*, viz., our passive condition).

Theology of the Person's Being

St. Thomas Aquinas made the breakthrough discovery. He saw that it is not the form, but the *act of being* (*esse*) of whatever is that is "the perfection of perfections." This insight, however, has not been well-integrated into an understanding of the person at the moment of creation *ex nihilo*.

Despite his reference to creation as *emanatio totius esse* (an emanation of the whole being), Thomas was overly invested in the dynamics of our cosmic existence.[15] He even thought that the body is gradually ensouled. His conception of the body as first having a vegetative soul, then an animal soul, and finally a rational soul shows a major weakness in the metaphysics, not just in the general science of nature.

So, while we continue to appreciate deeply the unprecedented discoveries of Aquinas in the philosophy of being, we cannot look to him for a breakthrough in an ontology of creation. St. Thomas' strong devotion to the viewpoint of the Aristotelian philosophy of nature and metaphysics (in which there can be no creation *ex nihilo*)—not to mention his early death at age 49—seems to have limited his metaphysical reflections on the *creation* of persons as *persons*.

His penetrating distinctions between various kinds of potency and act, based in prime matter, hold particular merit for seeing continuities in physical nature. His application of formal and material causality to sacramental

---

[15] The standard scholastic definition of creation as *productio rei ex nihilo sui et subjecti* reveals its weakness in the word "*productio*." God gifting being to unique created persons by an infinite act of love is *nothing like* a production, an effort, or a delivery—kinds of causality that are found only in cosmic existence.

and ecclesial matters is especially enriching. But much is missing.

People have difficulty, for instance, in believing that conception is the beginning of a human *person* in the cosmos. Many think that conception results only in a "potential person," instead of an *actual* person with great potential. Most tend to think, at least unconsciously, that there is no person there, only a tiny body. They fail to realize that all of this body, even as it grows, is specifically and necessarily an *essential part* of the *whole person* whose body it is.[16]

In the classical tradition, most critically, we have not differentiated carefully the *redemptive* or remedial creation from the *originative* creation. We are virtually unaware of ourselves as originatively perfect persons who are now struggling to recover from a partial and tragic denial of the supreme gift of being—a denial not only by Adam and Eve, but by each one of us. We are quite disposed to impede any reflection on the mere possibility of such a reality.[17]

---

[16] People often confuse *functional* potency and *natural* potency. Even as a zygote or embryo, this tiny being has the *natural* potency to read and write—something a rabbit embryo does not have and will never have. The *functional* potency to read and write for the human being and the *functional* potency to hop around and eat lettuce for the rabbit is what is missing. Not the natural potency. Entities are never to be identified merely according to functional potency, but according to natural potency: the intrinsic capacity of their essences for acting in specific ways for which they were created.

[17] We can carelessly write it off as being akin to the notion of Origen (d. c. 254 AD) or as being a new form of Gnosticism. But it is neither. Origen had a vague intuition, for which an ontological metaphysics would have served well, though it could only be developed over centuries. Gnosticism is a kind of knowledge that is considered accessible only to the privileged.

Yet originative sin is accessible to anyone with the ordinary gifts of faith and reason: an inescapable inference from the reality of our imperfect start

Theology of the Person's Being

We need to realize that we do not begin to *be* at conception. We begin, in effect, to *become*. Conception happens *to* us—to our ontologically fallen personhood.[18]

At the supreme, non-durational moment of being created out of nothing, we failed to *be* fully who we are; we caused our pristinely gifted *active receptivity* to fall into the ontological passivity, eventually known as the cosmos. So, our being conceived within our mother affords us the opportunity to come out of the coma of be-ing that resulted from our originative crash.

In space and time, then, we develop through our body as a whole. This physical area of our being constitutes a kind of "placenta of our potential salvation" by which our larger self extends into the cosmos and gestates its response to redemption.

We are thereby finally able to awaken and to become eventually aware of who we are, what happened, and the urgency of our condition before God. Yet, we encounter the multiplicity of blocks to consciousness, caused by our self-passivized nature.

When we look to issues at the origin of human life, for instance those surrounding conception, we are quite handicapped at first. The contemporary issues of abortion, *in vitro* fertilization, embryonic stem cell research, cloning, and other bioethical concerns are discussed

---

as created persons faced with God's infinite goodness and power. The reality of such sin is the only conclusion that affirms God's creating *will* as in no way arbitrary, much less tyrannical.

[18] No reincarnation is implied. Such would deny the essential integrity of the individual person. We fell once personally. Now we have only one opportunity to recover through the infinitely compassionate work of God involved in creation (not re-creation) *ex aliquo* and culminating in the life, death, and resurrection of the Word of God.

virtually in a metaphysical vacuum where the human *person* is missing.

We have failed in *be*-ing—in *do*-ing our *being*—and we have spiritually denied that we were ever personally gifted with a perfect being. So, we first think of the human being essentially as a "rational animal"—in the *genus* of animal.[19]

In reality, however, every human being is an intuitively-rational *person*—in the *genus* of *person*, along with *purely-intuitive* persons (the angels) and God.

Hylomorphism (matter-form theory) holds well for some of the basics of subpersonal entities and for mobile being in general, but it is a foundational disaster when applied to human persons. The idea of a totally immortal soul "informing" passive matter jolts the highly intuitive intellect. And unconsciously clinging to cosmological hylomorphism for appreciating our identity as *persons* has only encouraged the Cartesian cataclysm and the subsequent fracturing of soul and body, theoretically and practically.

---

[19] For an extended treatment of the devastating effects of thinking that the human being is a "rational animal" and for a positive person-based meaning, see the forthcoming work of Mary R. Joyce, *The Future of Adam and Eve: Power for Wisdom about Love* (St. Cloud, Minn.: LifeCom, 2008).

Six

Toward an Ontology of Creation

Attaining theistic renewal by deepening our traditional understanding of creation requires a unique frame of reference. We need to acknowledge the "missing person" in cosmological metaphysics, while attending to the primal significance of personhood as such.

Our perspective must *not* be even subtly cosmological, unconsciously assuming the framework of space and time concerning God's act of creating *ex nihilo*. Nor must it be object-oriented. It must be person-centered and "more than personal." It must be *inter*personal.

Yet an interpersonal viewpoint is difficult to hold. Even the promising phenomenological accounts offered today, concerned with person, relationality, gift giving, freedom, and so forth need a better ontological foundation. The implicit ontological framework, the essential structure of freedom and love, is crucial.

On the one hand, many modern philosophers made colossal epistemic blunders, trying to know *being* by first knowing *ideas* of being—in a vain attempt at a more "personal" knowing that was hardly more than noetic narcissism.

Facing the Dark Side of *Genesis*

On the other hand, many traditionalists had made a perennial mistake by starting with non-personal being (*Physica*), and then expecting to attain a significant insight into personhood, even while unconsciously dragging along that subpersonal frame of reference. They should have realized that contemplating the human soul or even a Prime Mover, while *unconsciously* committed to a mindset based in prime matter, is like tethering an eagle to the ground. No mere "judgment of separation" could suffice.

We need to move resolutely out of the "old realism paradigm" of fashioning, making, or forming an object and into the "new realism paradigm" of an *inter*personal giving-and-receiving of gifts. We can undertake to shift deliberately from cosmological metaphysics to ontological metaphysics, and from an unconsciously cosmocentric theology to ontocentric theology.[20]

This entry into an interpersonal perspective should include the time-honored Aristotelian recognition about *conscious* knowing. Although he did not always adhere to it, Aristotle articulated the principle that our conscious knowledge proceeds from that which is more knowable immediately to us (but less intelligible in itself) to that which is more knowable in itself (yet less intelligible immediately to us).

We ought to be more sensitive, however, and to realize that the lesser intelligibility cannot (by itself) lead us to the higher. The higher is ever actively present in the lower—even as it is known only through preconscious intuitive intellection.[21]

---

[20] Philosophers with some kind of an I-Thou theory, such as Buber and Marcel, have made good attempts, constituting a provisional beginning.

[21] Plato knew this truth implicitly—and without having to go into epistemological gymnastics so characteristic of our times. He also knew

Toward an Ontology of Creation

Most critically, we need to realize that the way we consciously *come to know* about our own human knowing itself is the reverse of the way the knowing actually works. When we come to know, for instance, a human act of knowing a tree *in its treeness*, we more readily come to know how the sensory aspects work. But, in the actual activity of knowing, these sensory aspects are secondary and subordinate to the intellective aspects, somewhat as parts are subordinate to the whole. These parts are necessary for conscious, rational knowing in the sensory world. But they are not necessary, even though viable, for us in knowing the world of being as such.

An ontological metaphysics begins with what is more intelligible in itself and not with passive matter and motion as such. It honors the role of the spiritual unconscious (the preconscious) that supremely conditions any human knowing in the ordinary world of consciousness. It centers on persons in giving-receiving relationships, the *essences* of which are active, not passive.[22]

---

that this world was inherently flawed. Such insight seems to be missing in Aristotle. Plato knew something was askew with the spatiotemporal world, even though he did not recognize an infinitely perfect God, nor an originatively perfect creation and the freedom of our interpersonal response. The Good, however, was considered somehow integrative of both suprasensible forms and individual manifestations.

Aristotle recognized the agent intellect as a necessary function of affording light for the workings of knowing, but not as itself a knowing power. Subconscious, unconscious, and preconscious knowing were largely unattended.

[22] Ontology—the study of *any* being as *being* (substance, accident, relation or whatever), *including supernatural being*—is only as good as it is open to divine Revelation. Even as the philosophy of nature is open to the data and conclusions of contemporary science, an ontological philosophy is open to the data and conclusions of faith, of science, and of everything else. This philosophy does serious and critical reflection without claiming to generate any of the data in religion or in scientific discovery. In its wisdom-bearing integration, this activity contributes pivotal, critical

Facing the Dark Side of *Genesis*

Therein the knower can develop a firm understanding of *receptivity* as radically different from the passivity that is so central to cosmological metaphysics and even to classical metaphysics itself.

In our ordinary discourse, receptivity is constantly thought of as passivity, or at least as partial passivity. But true receptivity is not at all passive. Originatively, receptivity is an *active* potency found (analogously) in both finite and *infinite* being. The latter kind of being is the "more than adequate" cause of the perfect finite.[23]

---

perspective to the *philosophies* of both science and faith (theology) and of any other kind of perspective on reality, such as psychology and sociology.

[23] In theology, the development of the meaning of *person* transpired amidst Councils of the Church struggling to defend basic doctrines, such as the Trinity and the Incarnation. Despite immense progress, theologians still suffer from the underlying philosophical cosmolock. The meanings for *hypostasis*, subsistent relations, and so forth were impeded by the lack of ontological consciousness of persons as essentially prior to any substance or subsistence in the spatiotemporal realm.

Fixation on the Aristotelian ten categories of being had its surreptitious sway, especially in the predicament known as *relation*. Thus, cosmological *relation*, known as the logical category—unwittingly engaged—tried to do service in the theological and ontological spheres while thinkers were deliberating over the transcendental aspects of being.

Besides, Boethius' definition of a person as *an individual substance of a rational nature* was haunting the premises and was never fully disengaged from the cosmological setting for *substance* and *rational*.

To be and *to be a person* is to be both unique and super-related to *all* else. Seeing anything less is the "work" of originative sin in the minds of philosophers.

In the end, people really are not called to worship "subsistent relations," but rather Persons who are infinite Gifts to one another and to us.

Seven

From Forming and Being-Formed to Giving and Receiving

The causality of the primal creation is an activity of both giving and receiving. It is not simply a "giving." God *gifts* us, both by giving us our be-ing and receiving our immediately free response. *Ex nihilo*, there is no forming and being-formed. God is not really a super-active efficient cause, forming us as passive effects. In originative creation, there is *no* passive potency.

The classic meaning for efficient causality does not apply at all to creation that is *originative* causality. Commonly, efficient causality is thought to be an activity whereby something (the effect) passively depends for its being—really, for its *existence* or for coming to *exist*—upon something else (the cause or causes).

But this meaning is based on the dependence of an effect upon its efficient cause, as situated in cosmic matter and motion. Finite causality, as exercised in this world of inherent defects, cannot really signify anything *intrinsic* regarding the infinite causality of God's *creation ex nihilo*.

Facing the Dark Side of *Genesis*

God originatively creates only perfect persons, not undeveloped ones. By our *defective response* to the gift of be-ing and of being perfect, we fallen humans *have made ourselves* to be in dire need of development. Redemption requires a process.

Our originative response to *being* was immediate, perfectly free, and unencumbered by temptation. As we were being created out of nothing, there was no room for being tempted by any person—other than ourselves. We faced God directly—not in divine glory, but nonetheless in real Being. And we *responded immediately and intimately* to the divine act alone. Interpersonal intimacy was at stake. Glory would have been ours, if we had said fully *yes*.

Even in the traditional theological framework, we might ask, "Who tempted Lucifer?" The obvious answer is *no one*. Faced immediately and intimately with God's being, we were not temptable by any other person.

After our sin, we remained persons essentially as God-gifted. Yet, as the result of our immediate, faltering primal reception, we have ravaged our side of the gift. So, we are imperfect beings by virtue of being *both* perfect *and* imperfect. We are not, so to say, simplistically and solely, imperfect.[24]

We are also now temptable—able to be *acted upon* by others in adverse ways. We created our temptability by our originative sin that caused our own passive potencies,

---

[24] Only material entities are simply imperfect. Broken dishes, chopped down trees, diseased plants and animals, and all manner of material substances are solely imperfect, having no *perfection* intrinsic to them. Spiritual entities, human beings and angels, however, retain their originative perfection, even when "broken" or imperfect. They are then imperfect by being *both* perfect *and* imperfect. They remain perfect as God's gifted beings, but they are imperfect as *received* by themselves.

From Forming and Being Formed

spiritwise and otherwise. God could not create *directly ex nihilo* kinds of being that were passive or temptable-by-others. Perhaps, we could say, at best, we originatively "tempted" ourselves.

The Adam and Eve of *Genesis* were temptable because they had already *untemptedly* said *maybe* to God. **Coming out of the "dark side of Genesis," Adam seemed to be so weak, so passive, that he did not offer the least resistance to the temptation.** He was the original wimp.

Moreover, the New Adam, Emmanuel, was not temptable. He *could not* sin. So, the temptations of Satan were trials. Jesus was tormented, yes. Tempted, no. Like us in all things, except sin and the *ability to sin*.

Critically important is the redeeming love that makes it possible for us to be saved from everlasting frustration. Yet, in order to be saved, we still have to *receive* this rescue of our being *by our own act of will*—our own self-determination.

Redemption comes to us without our conscious will. We, however, cannot attain *salvation*—fully intimate union with God forever—without our *willing* it. In saving us, infinite power and goodness respects our freedom to cooperate.

Moreover, we will have to do more than intense *wanting* to be saved. We will have to be actively *willing*—no matter what adversities might assail us from within and from without.

Salvation will finally render us fulfilled persons, *granted our sincerity in receiving it*. When we say, "I'm saved," how deeply sincere are we? How honestly do we believe?

Facing the Dark Side of *Genesis*

In any case, we will be fully affected forever, by our originative act. We will be those who *became* fulfilled persons (by way of redemption and salvation) in contrast to others of our kind who might have said, immediately and fully, *yes* to their gifted being and to their gifting Creator.

The latter are *simply* perfect persons. If we are sincerely *willing*, we will be *complexly* perfect persons: giftedly *being* perfect and receptedly *become* perfect.

Moreover, subpersons (animals, plants, *et al.*) are not part-persons. They are not persons at all. They are part-beings, not whole beings. They are created (*ex aliquo*) by God from the ontological *effects* of *our* originative sin—our first great act of personhood.[25]

This radical realization cannot be granted theologically by using merely cosmological metaphysics and its principles of "being." Nor can an idealistic or rationalistic posture serve as a base. But, through an ontological metaphysics, theology could make this clear.[26]

---

[25] Subpersonal beings are not themselves sinful or evil in any way. Matter is good and essentially receptive. What *caused* matter to be *passive* is evil: the *originative* sin itself. By this sin, we ourselves are the sole, ultimate cause of our passive condition. We created our passivity *ex aliquo*—out of our less than perfect willingness to receive our being.

[26] In *Romans* 8, St. Paul writes about all creation groaning and being in travail like a woman in childbirth. Theologians hence have known that what they called the whole of creation was affected by an *original* sin. But, in general, they were disinclined to offer any semblance of an explanation on how an ontological interpretation was needed. They lacked awareness of how an *originative* illness of will in all fallen humans causally connected these humans with the existence of the passive matter and motion of the whole cosmos in space and time. Originatively, sinning humans caused passive receptivity and the need for redemption, of which the cosmos is manifestly a part.

From Forming and Being Formed

Development of an ontology of gift-giving and gift-receiving could serve to provide light on the first pages of *Genesis*. The story begs for more light.

Besides, the making and being done to—the non-giving, non-receiving kinds of causalities of less-than-personal interactions—must be newly recognized largely as impediments. They serve to inhibit us from discerning the meaning of originative creation as an *inter*-personal kind of causality.

At the non-durational (spiritual and ontological) moment of creation, God gifts, not "makes." And the created person (the gift) immediately and actively receives—without "being done to," without any passivity involved. In that moment, infinite goodness and power gives created persons perfect being and perfect freedom—to be and do their own *be*-ing. They *are* their (finite) *be*-ing; they do not merely have it (*habens esse*).[27]

---

[27] The Thomistic and scholastic notion of a created person as *habens esse*, *having* his or her being—but not *be*-ing it—lies right at the heart of a latent pantheism in the tradition itself. We are so fearful of claiming to be God that we surreptitiously demean God's sheer gift to us of perfect finite being, by thinking it is a gift that we can *have* but not really *be*—otherwise we would be God.

Apparently, being is thought to be *not really analogous enough* to include both infinite and finite. The idea seems to be that God *is* being (*esse*); we simply *have* being (*esse*). *Esse* (being) is differentiated into two kinds: the kind that *is* it (uncreated) and the kind that merely *has* it (created)—despite desperate efforts to stay properly analogous in meaning.

It would be better to say it outright: God is *not* being, but God is *God's being*: infinite being. God is not "the fullness of being" nor are we the participants in some being (God's) that we are *not by essence*. There is no "fullness" at all about *unlimited* being (God). Fullness is a finite condition. We do not strictly participate in God's being, or in any kind of being other than our own—and that perhaps rather poorly.

Each of us *is* his or her be-ing, sheerly gifted to us. We are *our* being, a unique finite being—perfect as finite, even as God is perfect as infinite. If God were literally being, then we would have to be "parts" of the one

Facing the Dark Side of *Genesis*

Even in everyday *human* life, the gifts of true friendship do not restrict the recipient, but serve as unqualified affirmations of his or her being. There is no *quid pro quo* attitude, at least to the extent that the giving transcends "buddyhood" or mere companionship. The *giving* is done without any expectancy of "return," and the *receiving* is done without any strict *need* to repay.

In true friendship, we act like God, who gifts us with *being*—our own being to *do*—without any *need* for our worship "in return"—and who receives our response with infinitely unconditional love. Our lack of cooperation with infinite love is entirely our responsibility in the gift of definitive *freedom* to love.

Originatively, we are created to be friends with all other persons. And at the core of every genuine friendship is *love: willing the truest and best for self and all others, despite the cost.*

So, there can be nothing cosmological about creation *ex nihilo*. The order found in the cosmos is an indirect, derivative order at best, having to do with the redemption of fallen persons much more than with the free reception of a finite gift of being. The cost to God is the inconceivable suffering of the Word-of-God-Incarnate.

In creation *ex nihilo*, of course, there is neither *nihilo* nor *ex*. In creating persons, God does not "work with nothing" any more than "with something." And there is nothing from which to "*ex*." Each created person, as a perfectly whole, finite being, is an absolute *gift*, emanating *freely* from the Heart of God.

---

being that is—by "participation"—and *that* is a kind of pantheism. The *infinite power* of God to gift us with *our own perfect* beings is being implicitly denied or demeaned.

From Forming and Being Formed

This gift-being is the perfect whole of each created person—a perfect gift of God to the created self. The Giver is perfect, and so is the gift—in being, in being finite, and in *freedom to receive*.[28]

---

[28] Every person as a person, infinite or finite, is a gift. First of all, a gift to self. The gifting activity, whether to self or to another, is totally spiritual and the giving and receiving involved are not at all a "forming and being formed." They are a receivingly giving and a givingly receiving.

In the Trinity, the procession of Persons begins, so to speak, with the Father infinitely and eternally both giving and receiving Himself in gifting infinitely and eternally the Word Person, and so forth. Each Divine Person's infinite activity of *receiving* Self is just as real as the giving of Self.

The immense and beautiful struggle to develop the meaning of being a person and applying it to the doctrine of the Trinity, both in the East and in the West, suffers from the human fixation on the cosmos, such that receiving always seems to mean somehow, at least in part, something passive. The notions of the receiving of God by God and the receiving of created persons by God are difficult to appreciate. Our imprisonment in the cosmolock and in the lack of an adequately paradoxical logic makes these ideas "cast outs." Because *we* are "cast out" we discard such ideas. We do not want to face them, as they remind us vividly of the "dark side."

The paradox-power to see opposites as fully distinct, yet fully "interpenetrative," is missing. The immanence and transcendence of God, for instance, cannot be dealt with by a "paradoxical" logic that is basically compensatory, such as the yin-yang in Oriental thought, where the one member "makes up for" or complements the other—hot for cold, and vice versa; man for woman, and vice versa.

But God's immanence, for instance, does not "make up for" or balance God's transcendence. Both are "equal" and inter-receptive opposites. Underlying this and many other paradoxes of faith and reason is the paradox of true giving as a *receiving* kind of giving and true receiving as a *giving* kind of receiving.

Eight

Two Creations: Originative and Redemptive

Here in this world, we know and think from our "cast out" position—looking back toward the scene of expulsion. So, without realizing it, we are doing our thinking about two quite different divine creations.

For ages, religious and philosophical thinkers have been telescoping these two creations: the creation of the spatiotemporal universe, designed for the redemption of the cosmically confined, has been largely identified with the original (perfect) creation of persons, as persons only—angelic and human. Consequently, believers have been confusing rehabilitation with origination. Our becoming is blurring our being.[29]

The originative creation is the gift of being: gifted to persons as fully able to receive the gift with perfect freedom. Some did receive fully (notably the good angels). Others rejected fully. And still others (ourselves) were

---

[29] We might speak meaningfully of more than these two creations. For instance, the creation of sanctification would be a third kind, emphatically associated with God the Holy Spirit and occurring within the creation of redemption that is done incarnationally by God the Word. The latter creation itself occurs fully within the originative creation (emphatically attributed to God the Father).

Facing the Dark Side of *Genesis*

immediately ambivalent, creating a void, a darkness, and a passivity whereby we needed redemption in and from this unstable, self-alienating existence.[30]

By failing to receive fully and joyfully our own being, we hung ourselves between heaven and hell, and we need to choose definitively between salvation and damnation. By our originative act itself, along with repressing the act, we caused our ontological passivity and unconsciousness, from which we have been suffering.[31]

As imperfect receivers of being, we are now, thank God, in recovery: conceived and enwombed in this multiply-ambivalent cosmos. This is a *yes-no* world, a *maybe world*

---

[30] The originative creation is a gift of *being*—not at all a gift of *existence*. The common practice of using synonymously the terms *being* and *existence* should cease. Ex-istence should be referred to as a *kind* of being: an ontologically alienated kind. Whether it is the existence of a simply physical reality with quantitative extension, or the existence of the fallen human way of being—by standing consciously outside oneself in order to make choices—the word is heavily laden with implications of its etymology: being "standing outside itself." The elision of meaning involved in the words *being* and *existence* is, then, a prime way to hide from ourselves the originative sin—the sin in our faltering *response* to *being* that caused our *ex-istence*.

God and created persons in heaven do not *exist*. They simply *are*. God, infinitely; created persons, finitely. We could aid ourselves in recovery from atheistic tendencies by frankly admitting that God does not ex-ist. God *is*.

Nor is God hiding from us. God has "nowhere" to hide. By our primal sin in our beginning to *be*, we have tried to hide ourselves from God right within the divine intimacy. Ironically, we now plead, "Lord, where are *you*?"

[31] A woman who has aborted a child and denies that she was ever pregnant *can* remember her action. She aborted in space and time, accessible by memory. We, however, cannot *remember* our immediately free response to God, because our act of saying less than *fully yes* occurred in the non-durational moment of our beginning to *be ex nihilo*. That originative response helped to *cause* space and time to exist, but could not have been itself spatiotemporal. So, this sin is strictly inaccessible to memory, but quite available to recognition and knowledge.

of good (*yes*) and evil (*no*). In this kind of world we never know what tomorrow will bring. Maybe this or maybe that. This kind of contingency signifies imperfection, but not finiteness as such.[32]

Our immediate and partial *yes*, together with God's infinitely unconditional love, resulted in God's gift to us of becoming. We are now taking our one and only opportunity in space and time to recover from our ontological crash. We are called to muster, with divine grace, as much *yes* to our being and to God as we can. In this way, we show our willingness to come back—our sincerity of be-ing.[33]

Both creations—the redemptive and the originative—have been effected in and through the Word of God. The creation of becoming (as described in *Genesis*) is the redemptive or remedial creation (out of a void or out of prime passivity). And the original creation of *being*—the creation *ex nihilo* that was recognized by some of the early Fathers of the Church—should have been acknowledged as the creation of *perfect persons* (angelic and human) by the Persons of God. Instead, it was vastly assumed as the same one that *Genesis* described.

---

[32] Traditional philosophers and theologians have habitually claimed that to be finite is to be contingent. Yes, finite being is contingent being, as opposed to necessary being. Finite persons, however, as finite, are not necessarily imperfect. Imperfection brings on a new and *unnecessary* kind of contingency that is the hallmark of our spatiotemporal world.

[33] We can speculate that, at the non-durational moment of death, there could be a special final summons to receive Jesus, the Word, as Savior. While this would call for a uniquely free decision on our part, much of this final opportunity for a full *yes* would be founded on how well we did in the originative reception of our be-ing—how much *yes* and how much *no* in our *maybe*—as well as on how sincerely we lived in space and time, repentantly or unrepentantly.

Facing the Dark Side of *Genesis*

The creation of *becoming* might be said to be gestating within the creation of *being*—the originative, *immaculate creation.*

Nine

True Receiving Is Pure Activity

We are created persons who were originatively indecisive about being finite. Now we are laboring to know ourselves and to gain an ultimate perspective. Our traditional metaphysics, however, is freighted with the concept of passivity—something totally foreign to the initial creation.[34] We fail to realize that an infinitely perfect Being *could not* be arbitrary and so *could not* create—*ex nihilo*—anything passive, including "passive potencies."

With infinite intimacy, God creates directly only finite persons, who are perfectly able to receive the gift actively and intimately. The created person is gifted to *be,* to *be-with,* and to *act-with* God and all others—and *not* to be *acted upon* in any way.

Our failure fully to receive would *necessarily* have caused an immediate constriction of our being—freezing our receptivity into massive passivity. Our perfect power to receive-without-being-done-to, became loaded, by our

---

[34] In Thomistic theology and philosophy, even the essences of the good angels, who responded to their creation perfectly with perfect freedom, are thought to be passive. The essences of these angels are regarded as being in *passive potency* with respect to their own *acts* of being. This is a classic misapplication of cosmological terms to ontological determinations.

sin, with another power: the (imperfect) power to receive-by-being-done-to. Our *act* of exercising imperfectly the perfect power to receive-without-being-done-to caused us to have the imperfect power to receive. Purely active potency became largely passive potency. The passivity we now find inevitably in our potencies thereby comes from us, not from God.

We ought to cease confusing finite being with defective being. Otherwise, we will likely continue to maintain unconsciously our hesitancy about *receiving* our being.

To be finite is not necessarily to be defective. The good angels are ever perfect, finite beings. Like the angels, we were gifted originatively with a perfect finite being, not a defective one. We were perfect as gifted, though imperfect as received immediately by ourselves.

Unlike the angels, we were originatively *both* matter (pure receptivity, not passivity) *and* form. But we were perfectly active matter as well as perfectly active form. Perfectly active *receptivity,* as well as perfectly active *givity*.

Our kind of receptivity is double: a receptivity both of our essence for our being and of our essence for itself. The angels' superior receptivity is simply for being.

If we are going to improve our understanding of the first creation—the absolute beginning of our being—we must acknowledge it as a non-durational moment of supreme being-full (ontological) priority. Both angelic and human receivers of the gift of being are involved together. This

True Receiving

interpretation underlies, and is presupposed by, the explicit *Genesis* account.[35]

Likewise required is a discernment of the second creation as the beginning of our *becoming*. This creation was initiated by divine Mercy at the same non-durational moment as the origin of our being. We were created, and immediately multitudes of persons like ourselves failed to receive *fully* the absolute gift of being. God responded *immediately* by creating our *becoming*.

The creation of *becoming* has been given a functional and partial description in *Genesis*. But this second or remedial creation has been perennially conflated with creation *ex nihilo* (the creation of *being*), from which the ultimate dynamics of both creations emanate.[36]

Contemporary debates on creation, such as those between creationists and evolutionists, are conducted as though they deal with absolute origins. Instead, the participants are sparring over the creation of becoming, not of being. Both creationists and evolutionists are fixed on process or becoming. For creationists generally the process tends to be six days; for evolutionists it might be six eons.[37] Origins that admit of any kind of process cannot be primary origins.

---

[35] Without disparaging Augustine's particular anagogical interpretation of the Scriptural text, we must get into an ontology of both finite and infinite persons.

[36] The theological struggle, in Jewish and Christian sources, even to recognize creation *ex nihilo* is delineated by Gerhard May, *Creatio ex Nihilo: The Doctrine of "Creation out of Nothing" in Early Christian Thought* (Edinburgh: T & T Clark, 1991). His interpretation seems to be subject to serious question, at least with respect to various Biblical texts, such as 2 *Maccabees* 7:28.

[37] Some classical thinkers, even in the absence of contemporary scientific data and methodology, had a far better perspective. St. Augustine proposed that God created everything in one "day," including the "package of

Facing the Dark Side of *Genesis*

Both sides overlook, or seem to be unaware of, creation *ex nihilo*, the necessarily free and immaculate creation of finite persons, having nothing as such to do with process, time, and space. Creationists, especially, think they are speaking of God as creating out of nothing by way of a process. Unconsciously, God is thereby deemed to be a Magician. But nothing *imperfect* can *be* by the sole activity of God directly "out of nothing."[38]

If we do well our work of creation-ontology, we can come to see that, since subpersonal creatures (from molecules to monkeys) cannot freely receive the gift of being, they do not belong within the originative creation of persons, including human persons. They fit exclusively in the creation of becoming. They were created to support redemption's graduative purpose for fallen humans: that these persons might *become* whom they were originatively created to *be*. By God's redemptive love, all subpersonal being has been created *ex aliquo*—out of the mega-energy generated by the (partial) *yes* of our collective *maybe*.[39]

---

powers" (*rationes seminales*) out of which all subsequent existents would eventually emerge. Even earlier, Origen had a glimmer of an ontological perspective on the origin of evil in fallen humans, without the philosophical resources to give a plausible account.

The question of the absolute origins of human kind or any kind cannot be resolved by either a creationistic or an evolutionistic approach. Both sides fail to appreciate the nature of the search. The determination could only be made ontologically and theologically, with the critical help of truly scientific development and of prayerful reception of genuine Revelation.

[38] God's infinite power makes it possible and God's infinite goodness makes it necessary that every originative creature be perfect in being and freedom.

[39] The anthropic principle, broadly taken, goes back to Aristotle. In various forms, however, it has become seriously entertained by some scientists in our own times. The general idea is that all of the cosmos is so structured that it anticipates the coming of the human. (Continued, next page.)

True Receiving

Neither the Eastern nor the Western world has a "good record" on understanding the activity of *receiving*. The meaning of receptivity is haunted by the meaning of passivity.

A classic principle in medieval philosophy states that whatever is received is received according to the mode of the receiver. The receiver receives according to *its* "nature." A sieve receives water like a sieve, letting most of the liquid fall through. A cup receives water like a cup, holding the liquid in place.

This concept is taken from cosmically passive things that are almost totally passive. Oriental wisdom, suggests the involvement of a person, in the idea of trying to receive what is received, according to the nature of that which is received. We clean a dish thoroughly in order to receive milk, as milk *is*, and not as contaminated by fruit juice coating the cup from an earlier usage. Analogously, "the enlightened one" is someone who purges his or her mind, the better to receive without tainting the message received.

But in these perspectives the emphasis is on "being done to," for better or for worse. The activity of receiving is assumed to be both a doing and a being-done-to. *That* is the condition of a redemptive creation, a recovery after the "crash."

I am claiming that there is an intrinsic reason for this, since *all* of energy and passive matter result from the originatively indecisive response of humans to *creation ex nihilo*. In creation *ex aliquo* (redemptive creation), cosmic matter anticipates human being and telically tends toward it. Why? Because, in its passive-reactive form as energy, and as an effluent of the crash in originative human freedom, this energy already had come from mangled human freedom. Such energy is creative only because of God's redeemingly creative love within it.

Facing the Dark Side of *Genesis*

Originative, purely active receiving that we "*do* without being done-to" is the God-like receiving to which we are called. We try to be-*with* God and do-*with* God the *receiving* of all being as it is, not as we want it to be.

Ten

The Redemptive Creation

We can hardly over-emphasize that God creates directly (*ex nihilo*) *persons only*. Subpersons (minerals, plants, animals) are created, by God's redemptive love, out of *something*: out of energy, that results from our *no-yes* (passive-reactive) response to *being*.[40]

Energy came from the faltering of human persons, as they exercised their pristine freedom. Energy is inherently defective. *Yet it is also* part of God's redemptive means for our recuperation and recovery. Even sacred actions rely, for their signs, on energy as physical matter—in words, water, oil, and so forth. Sacraments are "incarnational."

Energy is a "precipitate" of the originative crash. It is the capacity to do work—especially the work of cooperating with God's *infinitely active* (redemptive) response to the *yes* part of our *defective* receiving of originative creation.

Energy without divine power would be chaotic. Its implosive dimension is passive and constrictive. Its explosive dimension is reactive. Together with God's

---

[40] The term *energy*, as used in this essay, is not the same as that used by physicists and other empirical scientists. But the meaning is highly related analogically and would fit within ontological reflections on the philosophy of nature.

infinitely responsive power, energy expresses itself in the super-fragmentive and spatialized matter of the whole cosmos.

All energy is paradoxical: both passive and active. It originates from the *no-yes* of *maybe*-saying, initially done by multitudes of human persons. Their *no* reduces receptivity to *passivity*. The *yes* causes reaction, and God's love is *responsive* to the *yes*: constituting a passive-reactive-responsive union of human energy with divine power.

God is, in no way, energy. There is no such thing as "divine energy." God is infinite power, without any passivity. Yet, divine power is not so much "power-over," but "*unlimited* power-*with*," in which we can finitely share as being-*with* God.

The first creation was done by infinite-power, without any energy involved. The second (redemptive) creation included energy, the immediate (internal) source of cosmic matter.

Philosophically defined as the capacity to do the work of *existence*, energy is an implosive and explosive *reaction* to the fall of our active receptivity into passivity at the origin of our being. The self-demeaning of our being and of our freedom caused the passive-reactive condition with which God infinitely acts to restore fallen creation.

God's *power* allows the intensification, direction, and ordering of fallen humans' implosive-explosive *energy*. But the immense temporal lagging of activity and development comes solely from the originatively and continuously ill will, caused by created persons—human and satanic. God does God's infinite part. But we fallen humans must do our finite part.

The Redemptive Creation

From planets to plants, and from atoms to animals, and so forth, degrees of (subpersonal) likeness to human persons were formed gradually within this divinely-engaged energy. In all forms of energy, a teleological structure is found. Every particle of matter is to some degree constituted by the reactive thrust of the dynamics of becoming toward the redemption of human persons.[41]

Adam is the leader in this second (redemptive) creation. The first creation was perfect, even though hierarchical, in its kinds of finite personhood.

For Lucifer and his cohorts, however, redemption is not possible. Nor is it possible for some humans, if they said, in all their originative freedom, fully *no*. Because of their unqualified refusal to receive the gift, their response is not even a partial *yes*, with which redemptive and salvific activity could work.

An ontological account of creation-sin-redemption would elucidate the radically personal freedom and responsibility of every finite person as a person-in-community—angelic and human.

We need renewal of our theistic minds and hearts. Then we can find relief from our "creation conflation" and from the repression of our personal responsibility for being here in this world of good and evil.

---

[41] The fractuality (fractured actuality) of human *freedom* caused by the ontological crash would seem to have taken two basic forms: freedom imploded and freedom exploded. The results of the ontological *implosion* of our freedom would have ministered to our eventual, personal *bodily* constitution. The ontological *explosion* would have turned out to be our particular personal "*contribution*" to the fractuality known as the impersonal energy of the whole cosmos. Fractured personal *freedom* cannot be measured or confined.

Eleven

Consequences for Our Lives of Faith

The change within the Christian worldview suggested by the Perfect Creation Viewpoint is significant. But it is obviously not essential for salvation. No new doctrine of Faith or dogma is implied. Simply, the need is for deeper dimensions, with better theological focus and meaning.

This new view is basically *an intensification and magnification of belief* in creation and in the origin of evil. It purports to enrich some of the main theological concepts within the tradition.

Christians have believed throughout the ages that God is infinite in perfection. Many have also been taught that all have sinned somehow through the defect in human nature that comes from the sin of Adam and Eve.

Catholics believe this original sin was inherited. Other theists believe our faulty start is circumstantial, coming as it does after the sin. But all believe we are sinful people.

The new perspective affords somewhat deeper roots for understanding God's perfect creation and the origin of evil. The absolute beginning of evil, committed by many angels and human persons, is set at the creature-side of the singular moment of creation *ex nihilo,* and not in a

Facing the Dark Side of *Genesis*

spatiotemporal or quasi-cosmic condition of earliest beginnings.

Traditional belief holds that we are sinners because we are members of Adam's fallen nature. The new view says *yes*. But it is even truer to say that we are in the community of Adam only because we have previously sinned, together with him. Such is the other side of the doctrine of original sin and its consequences. Original sin is understood to be rooted in *originative* sin that is ontological and much more *personal*.

The deeper-roots perspective is an attempt to specify what happened at the primal origin of our *being*, and to show that the events of *Genesis* do not directly reveal that origin. The new view exposes, instead, our latent, spiritually repressed knowledge not only of our *becoming*, but of our *being*. This view is an attempted discernment of the ontology that is implied in the accounts and the wisdom of Sacred Scripture, as well as in the whole theistic tradition.

God's creation resulting in less than perfect being, such as we find in *Genesis*, is seen to be rooted in an *originative, immaculate creation* that is caused by God alone. This *ex nihilo* creation is essentially interpersonal for both Creator and created, in which the infinitely free Persons of the Trinity absolutely *gift*, into being, perfectly free finite persons, who are *necessarily able* to respond freely and immediately.

In addition to moral renewal, we need an ontological awakening in faith.[42] The impact might have to be

---

[42] Traditional thought, generally, does not distinguish well between the doing of our *being* and the doing of our *behavior*. Ontological sin would seem to be absurd. Thinkers concentrate on what could be called this sin's total effects in the various ways of human behavior and intent. But

Consequences for Our Lives of Faith

disturbing, at first, somewhat like the psychoanalytic awakening within twentieth century psychology and medicine, where repression as a fact was vehemently resisted, and yet was finally taken seriously. Light on the depth of unconscious motivation was a new horizon that now enriches the study of the human psyche, despite the atheistic and agnostic contexts of its origins.

Similarly, the new ontological view highlights the prospects of there being a spiritual unconscious (preconscious) life. In the depths of the preconscious mind, we know the actuality of our faltering at the pristine moment of receiving our being, but we hold it repressed.[43]

---

originative sin, the ultimate cause of evil in our lives, remains outside the focus of attention.

Because we regard creation in a latently material way, we think God does all the "being," that is, by giving us our being, handing it over like a delivery; and then we do not *be* our being, but use it, well or poorly. Our passive-mindedness cannot fathom our actively *receiving*, and being fully responsible for, our own being by *doing* it.

[43] It may require considerable phenomenological analysis in order to reveal our originative sin. But there are signs of the possibility.

Jacques Maritain brought out the power of the spiritual unconscious: the preconscious area of knowing that is indigenous to creativity. In his groundbreaking book on the creative process, he includes analysis of the power of the agent intellect. He calls this divine-like power within us the "Illuminating Intellect, a spiritual sun ceaselessly radiating." J. Maritain, *Creative Intuition in Art and Poetry* (N.Y.: Meridian Books, 1958), p. 73.

In the Thomistic tradition, this power is pure act in the order of intellection or "intelligibility-rendering." Unfortunately, Maritain did not recognize fully the power of this noetic agency. He repeated the Thomistic notion that the agent intellect is not itself a *knowing* power.

In reality, however, the agent intellect *knows immediately and preconsciously the being* of whatever is known. In the realm of our personal knowing it is like God in the order of being. God is the uncaused cause of our being. Our agent intellect is the uncaused cause of our knowing activity itself as a *knowing*. Surely, such a cause *knows* in a super-eminent manner, even as God *is* in a super-eminent manner. (Continued, next page.)

Facing the Dark Side of *Genesis*

It is my hope that the supposition of a Perfect Creation will give believers deeper and richer grounding in their faith—deeper than the usual cosmotheological approach to origins and destiny.

There would seem to be nothing in the new view to contradict the old. But the new can serve to face the traditional theology with prospects for intensifying and magnifying its meanings in the interest and care of the community of believers.[44]

Traditional thinkers, moreover, have entirely passed over the spiritual complement to agent intellect: *agent will*, the purely active power to love "with one's whole heart" God and all creation. *By that power of consummate self-determination*, we seem to have repressed considerably the noetic power of agent (active) intellect and totally repressed that agent will-power itself. It seems to be "a case of the missing power." We will not admit the reality of the power by which we committed originative sin. By that power we have repressed that power.

Perennially, knowing has been regarded as exclusively a function of a passive potency. The "possible or potential intellect," however, cannot possibly effect a knowing that is purely intuitive; nor can it be the complement or correlative for a purely active potency to love (agent will).

Maritain took some of his cues from the seminal work of Sigmund Freud concerning the reality of the *psychological* unconscious—the emotional underground of everyday life. I am claiming that the *spiritual* unconscious holds vast reaches of meaning at the depths of our being, wherein the originative, if partial, denial of our being occurred. Moreover, the importance for human meaning at the level of *emotionally* unconscious drives (Freudian) is minimal compared to the impact of our disordered *spiritual* drive that tends strongly to conceal from us our first act of *be*-ing and *mean*-ing.

[44] In the 20th century, breakthroughs have occurred on the meaning of *being* and on the reality of the unconscious. Especially helpful is the development of Thomism on the meaning of being, along with the enrichment of contemporary psychology by the systematic attention to the unconscious.

Acknowledging the *spiritual and ontological* dimensions of the unconscious (agent intellect and agent will) is only an intuitive step away from seeing that *be*-ing is *our* most important *act* and that our intellectual-volitional life had to be the ultimate practical source of the psychic life.

Consequences for Our Lives of Faith

Any debates would be about how to interpret Revelation theologically and philosophically. They would not deny the supernaturally gifted Revelation itself. We are due for more reasonworthy treatment of the legacy of faith. And every believer deserves a better response to the meaning of evil than saying, for instance, it is simply a "mystery" beyond our understanding.

There need be no dispute about basic truths of faith and reason. The explication of them, however, deserves our best attempts to provide an ever more coherent whole.

In order to show what is at stake in theology, several examples of the difference within the Christian worldview will have to suffice.

1. Which view affords a deeper look into Jesus as our *personal* Savior?

a. The traditional view that says Jesus redeems all of us from our personal sins and especially from our inherited original sin, forced upon us by our first parents and *their* history-making sin?

b. Or the new view that says Jesus redeems each of us from our sins and especially from our own personal originative sin, that we committed *within* the heart of God at the moment we were gifted with being? This pivotal sin was effected by us, along with Adam and Eve, our first parents in this redemptive world, and along with all persons who eventually become descendants of this first pair.

While less intelligible to us at first, the intellectual-volitional life is most intelligible in itself. If we are markedly influenced by unconscious motivation at the psychic level, all the more are we influenced by unconscious motivation in our spiritual and ontological depths. (We seem to have plenty of unconscious motivation to keep from ourselves our originative sin.)

Facing the Dark Side of *Genesis*

The origin of evil—our *interpersonal*, direct, free, untempted, *diffident* response to God—is an intelligible mystery in which we can participate more and more by knowing, loving, and repenting within it.

Each of us is the ultimate cause—but not always the immediate or even remote cause—of any and all evil that afflicts us. If we had not sinned originatively, we would not be *here*, where we are being "done to" and ultimately can be "done in" by our passivity in relation to adversarial forces of various kinds.

But we are most inclined to deny that it is so. We blame Adam and Eve, and Satan, consciously. And perhaps God, unconsciously.

Jesus comes to save, from personal sin, each one of us—even prebirth babies, whose originative sin is just as real as that of Adam and Eve. We are redeemed from *both* originative sin *and* the original sin in the Garden for the sake of our everlasting happiness and union with the three divine Persons.[45]

2. Which view helps us better to understand the *reason* for bad things happening to good people?

a. The traditional view that says bad things happen to good people because they were born into a world of the original sin of their first parents?

After creating angels, God "decided" to create a material world with first parents who just might "do in" themselves and all others who follow them. God's commitment to His

---

[45] The Sacrament of Baptism is conferred in the name of these three Persons. Such sacred action is understood as removing the stain of original sin. In the alternative view, this truth is given a "three-dimensional" perspective. The activity of baptizing, in the new view, would be regarded as a cleansing that is even more directly *personal* and intimate.

Consequences for Our Lives of Faith

original intentions prohibits Him from stepping in and preventing the many from contracting sin from the one, Adam. But the One Man, Jesus, comes to redeem us all.

b. Or the new view that says we failed by only partly receiving God's infinite gifting of being (creation *ex nihilo*)? From that originative sin, we all need redeeming and saving by an infinitely intimate personal Savior. We not only did inherit Adam's sin, but we *fully deserved* to inherit it.

Bad things happen to good people in this life because we are not as good as we think we are. And we continue to deny our ultimate responsibility for being here in this way.

3. Which attitude is more mature? Why *me*? Or why *not* me?

a. The traditional view sees unfairness and injustice everywhere in the world, without questioning how such a world realistically originated for *each* of its participants. As a result, at least subconsciously, each one asks, "Why *me*?" Especially, when tragedy strikes.

b. The new view sees everything happening as justice in its own way, despite the apparent levels of unfairness "on top." Everything that happens—whether good or evil—is a matter of justice at its root. It stems from the primal reception at the moment of creation *ex nihilo*. Each one can then ask, "Why *not* me?" If I committed the enormity of an originative sin, what manner of calamity could possibly be unjust?[46]

---

[46] The suffering of Jesus, our Redeemer, is paradoxical. Just and unjust. It is just in that it was necessary for saving from everlasting frustration those who would be willing to be saved. Jesus is infinite Justice and Mercy. But the world that put the Word of God through this unimaginable torture, within and without, teems with injustice. He who was sinless was "made sin" for our sake.

Facing the Dark Side of *Genesis*

4. Which theistic worldview is more opposed to the modern and contemporary self-centered notion of knowledge ("me no see, it no be")?

a. The traditional view that tends to identify knowledge as consciousness, reluctantly taking into account the subconscious and unconscious emotional or psychic life, as well as offering little realistic room for there being any repression in the *spiritual* life?

b. Or the new view that sees our conscious knowledge as the "tip of the iceberg"? Below the surface that we call consciousness, realms of *knowledge* are affirmed to *be* that are subconscious, unconscious, preconscious, and even protoconscious (at our originative reception of *being*). These areas of being are ever exerting powerful impacts on our attitudes and destiny. They need "consciousness-raising."

This latter theistic worldview admits we are repressing much of our lives in the physical, emotional, mental, and spiritual structures of our being. Redemption and salvation are considered to be, among other things, activities that finally rescue—from its frozen character of passive potency—our originative *purely active* potencies to know and love, our agent intellect and agent will.

5. Which inclination to pray is truer to our condition?

a. The common one that takes itself rather literally in saying, "God, *have* mercy on us," tending to pray as though God is *not* infinitely active and ever-present mercy necessarily, but is supposed to be moved to direct divine mercy here and there according to our prayer?

b. Or the new one that encourages more emphatic receptivity in praying? "God, I *receive* your infinite, ever-

Consequences for Our Lives of Faith

present mercy more deeply, on behalf of myself and others who may not be receiving You." Such prayer opens to the unlimited mercy of God that we know is instantly available everywhere and that seems to be constantly neglected and disrespected by us recovering self-aholics.

"Failures in mercy" are always failures to *receive* deeply and sincerely enough.

6. Which view lends greater support to us in our ability to repent and to change our lives?

a. The traditional view that seems to claim we are necessarily dependent on God *both* for salvation *and* for doing our very being?

b. Or the new view that holds we are necessarily dependent on God for salvation, but cannot be saved by infinite love unless we exercise our beingful power to be independent-*with* God?[47]

---

[47] Traditional theology seems to have worked with only two alternatives. The logic-lock of practical two-valued, unparadoxical thinking has prevailed. We are thought to be *either* dependent *on* God *or* independent *of* God. But an ontological meaning is being overlooked.

We are, at our creation *ex nihilo*, gifted to be independent-*with* God. Such is far from what we caused ourselves to be, at least partially, that is, independent *of* God. That self-caused "independence" rendered us totally dependent *on* God to recover our being. But the originative gift of being must have been one of being independent-*with* God.

Independence with respect to God is the only beingful basis on which we can personally *will ourselves* to be *open* to God's grace of redeeming life. As long as there would be even the *slightest* dependence in *being*, full and genuine intimacy with God would be impossible. And paradoxically, even the slightest dependence on ourselves would make salvation impossible.

We have confused our super–*relationship* to God with our super-*dependency* on God. Our sin blinds us to the gifting causality of God in creating us, whereby we are *not* rendered dependent, as we are in the defective causalities known within redemptive and recuperative existence. We are gifted with independent, finite being, designed to be-*with* God immediately and forever. (Continued, next page.)

Facing the Dark Side of *Genesis*

We are doing our own very *be*-ing—either well or not so well. *Doing it* means that we are *receiving* it from God and giving it to self and others, especially God. We *do* our being with the result that we can decide *independently* to be dependent on God for salvation. Thereby *we* let God bring us back to (be-come) the perfect whole being-*with*-God that we were originatively created to be. Or we can refuse to let God save us. In our pride, we can prefer self-destruction.

In any case, we are now all survivors. We have managed to endure a partial *self*-abortion at the moment of creation *ex nihilo*. Preconsciously, we all know this. But we tend to react instinctively by denial. We deny our responsibility for our own ex-istence—our manner of being somewhat alien to ourselves.

True repentance can include, at least implicitly in this present life, grievous regret for the originative rupture in the covenant of creation. By living in profound sorrow for originative sin and in ever deeper joy over our *personal* Savior, we can find liberation as a child of the infinitely merciful God.[48]

Again, our conflation of the two creations keeps us from knowing consciously our originative condition: being *finitely* independent-*with* the Persons of the Trinity, who are *infinitely* independent-*with* (inter-related with) One Another. In the "image and likeness" of the Triune Persons, we were originatively created.

[48] We shy away from thinking of creation as an interpersonal act whereby God's infinitely perfect act of creating us *necessarily* intends our immediately free response. Similarly, we are disinclined to think of Scripture as dialogic and interpersonal, requiring a supremely active response from the hearers. We tend to be passive receivers of the meaning, and to "think about it." But, perhaps, our first response in hearing the basic message of Revelation ought to be a personal admission of our originative sin that made redemptive creation necessary.

Much of Scripture, for instance, is reportorial, declarational, and proclamational. And we are asked, implicitly at least, for a full-hearted

Consequences for Our Lives of Faith

Other contrasts can be drawn between the traditional theological interpretation of Revelation and its extension by the new view. These differences would involve facing the real infinity of God, at all times and in all ways. In effect, we would be further encouraged to acknowledge our perfect freedom and responsibility for *doing our own being-with* God—an originative grace and gift, yet to be fully received.

---

response. Does not the fullness of revelation call for our actual, if implicit, admission that each one of us is personally involved in *why* we are here in space and time—*why* we are gifted with the Revelation at all?

Our responsibility includes somehow not only the *original* sin in the Garden that is personal to Adam and Eve and that has been reported. But, we are also, and preeminently, responsible for our personal *originative* sin. In a certain sense, the latter cannot really be merely reported, but must be personally *admitted*, before we can be received into realms of glory. The "report" of *this* sin should come *from us*. We can heartily acknowledge and implicitly declare our originative sin through living a sincerely repentant life, whether our knowledge of the depth of sin becomes conscious or not in this life.

Twelve

The Light on *Genesis*

The new light on *Genesis* is an ontological—not cosmological, not metaphysical, not simply theological—*affirmation* of the infinite perfection of God in accord with supernatural revelation. Ontology means starting our thinking from the unmediated knowing of being as *being*—not as a concept from cosmology or as an "*a priori*" dragged in unconsciously from a derivative kind of knowledge.

In no way does this light come *from* the senses. Even if we do not know it consciously, we are conceived with this light, born with it, live with it, die with it, and go with it into everlasting life or death.

The light of being is at least a bit conscious when we become aware that we are actually knowing the *being* of anything simply as *this unique being*—and as radically other than nothing. In such primal light, we see that God is *not* "being *itself*." Otherwise, *this*, and we, would not really *be*.

God *is God's* Being: Trinitarian, infinite, and eternal. The essence of God is not simply to be, but to be infinite and eternal. And we see that *we* are not "being *itself*." We

Facing the Dark Side of *Genesis*

are our being: triadic, finite, and everlasting by the grace (the being-with-us) of God.

Together with the light of faith, we know that the perfection of infinite being is infinitely interpersonal (Trinitarian), and that the *effects* of the primal creation by such being would have to be perfect and interpersonal *only*. Neither subpersonal nor apersonal.

An interpersonal creation means that God unlimitedly and unconditionally *both* gifts us with our perfect finite being *and* infinitely receives us. Our part includes actively and purely receiving the gift of who we are and giving ourselves fully to the Gifter. That requires consummate *active* receptivity.[49]

We can surely know that such receiving and giving cannot be automatic, but must be freely willed, if truly interpersonal. Then we can see that the originative "choice" can only be—ultimately—between *willing* to be finite and *willing* to be infinite.

Readers who truly think ontologically, that is, from the light of being as *being*, will be able to see new light on the dark side of *Genesis*. They will be able to know that the void and darkness in the beginning is something that indicates the *origin of evil* as a condition for the creation

---

[49] Most of us think that we are totally dependent on God for our being as well as for salvation, and that if God were to stop knowing us (a hypothetical contrary to real possibility) we would cease to be. That notion, however, implies chronic dependency in *being*, a form of pantheism, and regards us as functions of God. Rather, we would go right on doing our *be*-ing, so absolute and infinitely unqualified is the act of creating us *out of nothing*.

God's *infinite love* for us *gifts* us with a being that is entirely ours, to be independent-*with* God and all others. We were gifted (graced) to be neither dependent *on* God nor independent *of* God. Our dignity is in neither identity with God nor separation from God. It is all in the *with*, the relating, the willingness to love.

The Light on *Genesis*

of the cosmos. Realizing our failure in the originative creation, believers will penetrate more deeply into the mystery of evil.

The origin of evil and its pervasiveness in our world will have a *reasonworthy* answer and will not be such a huge enigma, relegated to the "obscurity of God." Some readers might even be willing to acknowledge themselves as the *sole ultimate cause* of the darkness *in their own lives*.

Evil could be seen in a new light: in the light of the perfect gift of God that we *are*. We will always be uniquely perfect gifts of God. Our perfect beingful giftedness will be an intrinsic standard, either for our everlasting happiness or for our everlasting misery.

In order to *receive* ourselves *fully* as being giftedly perfect forever, and despite our self-wrought, "disvalue added" imperfections, we are called into the depths of repentance right within God's infinitely merciful love.

*****

Robert E. Joyce, Ph.D. is *professor emeritus* of philosophy
St. John's University, Collegeville, Minnesota.

Responses to this book, *Facing the Dark Side of Genesis*, are particularly welcome. Please send comment, critique, or questions by email to robertjoyce@charter.net or to the home address below. Thank you.

Additional copies may be ordered from Lifemeaning.com.

About the Author

Robert E. Joyce is *professor emeritus* of philosophy at St. John's University in Minnesota. He received a B.A. in philosophy from the University of St. Mary of the Lake, Mundelein, Illinois, 1957; an M.A. in philosophy from De Paul University, 1960; and a Ph.D. in philosophy from International College, 1978. Doctoral studies were also done at the University of Notre Dame, 1959-61, where he served with a Teaching Fellowship, 1959-61, and as instructor of philosophy, 1961-62. He has taught philosophy also at De Paul University, Loyola University, the College of St. Benedict, and at St. John's University, 1962-94. At St. John's he spent some years as Director of the Tri-College Honors Program and as Chair of the Philosophy Department.

Dr. Joyce is the author of five books and numerous articles in scholarly and popular publications.
He and his wife, Mary, published the first pro-life paperback in the United States, *Let Us Be Born: The Inhumanity of Abortion* (Chicago: Franciscan Herald Press, 1970). In the same year, they also published an introduction to the philosophy of man and woman, *New Dynamics in Sexual Love: A Revolutionary Approach to Marriage and Celibacy* (Collegeville, Minnesota: St. John's University Press, 1970). Robert's doctoral dissertation was published in 1980 by the University of America Press. *Human Sexual Ecology: A Philosophy and Ethics of Man and Woman* has been used by several leaders in the natural family planning movement.

A Call for Input to Meet the Challenge of Creation Conflation

In another book, *Affirming Our Freedom in God: The Untold Story of Creation* (St. Cloud, Minn.: LifeCom, 2001), I attempt to develop a beginning ontology of creation, highlighting creation *ex nihilo* as necessarily an interpersonal act of giving and receiving being. Discussed are at least some of the major ontological consequences that such an understanding yields.

Mary Rosera Joyce, my spouse and colleague, has contributed significantly to my work. Deeply valued is her decisive thinking on the dynamics of ontological insight, on the devastating effects of the "rational animal" definition, and on the remedy of repositioning the human being in the *genus* of person. Also, critically helpful are her specific insights connected with the concept of energy as passive-reactive. Along with her editorial assistance, these and other ideas are gratefully received.

I am interested in gaining various other responses to the new perspective that is briefly introduced above in the present book, *Facing the Dark Side of Genesis*. The ideas in this book will be considerably developed and amplified in a large forthcoming volume: *When God Said Be, We Said Maybe: An Inside Story of the Creation, the Crash, and the Recovery* (St. Cloud, Minn.: LifeCom, 2009).

Any observations, suggestions, or objections will be given careful attention. Also, any relevant material, such as suggested references to phenomenological accounts of giving or receiving acts—descriptions or analyses—would be welcome.

I also encourage dialog by email.

Robert E. Joyce, Ph.D.
Professor Emeritus
St. John's University
Collegeville, Minnesota

Home address   1248 N. 13th Ave. St. Cloud, MN 56303
Website   www.Lifemeaning.com

Phone   320-252-9866
email   robertjoyce@charter.net

Glossary

Coming to Terms. The new theistic view requires an adventure in revisiting traditional terms. Faith and reason need an increase in depth-perspective on perennial truths.

Painters, for instance, once rendered their images in largely flat, two-dimensional presentations. They seemed to be unable to know how to represent the third dimension successfully. Similarly, because of a cosmological crunch, traditional philosophy and theology tend to be two-dimensional in presenting the great truths. If possible, our effort here is to change *not the truths, but the perspective* for the sake of better vision.

The following definitions and delineations of key terms might assist the reader's thinking about prospects for a better theistic view. These words and phrases are analogical, not univocal. They do not have one single, exclusive meaning. For brevity and practicality, however, only one or two main meanings are set down for each term.

God is the infinite Being of three Persons, who gifted all created beings to *be*. God is not merely perfect, all-good, and all-powerful. God is *unlimitedly* so. God is not a "whole being"; God is unlimitedly unique being.

Being and Becoming

Being (*ens*) can mean the totality of a given being: who or what it is. But, more specifically, be-ing (*esse*) is the *act*uality of being-at-all. Be-ing is the most important *act* of a whole being. All other acts and actualities, such as thinking, drinking, walking, talking, *et al*. are "branches of the act of be-ing." Somewhat counter to the traditional theism, being is regarded, in this book, as what we *are* and *do*. Be-ing is the gift God gives us to *be* and to *do*. *We* do our being. God does not. Being is an act, not merely a fact.

We do not simply "have" being. We *are* the entire be-ing God gifted us uniquely to *be* and to *do*. No part of our being is *of* God or *of* anyone else. We are fully and forever our own unique being, thanks to the *infinitely* powerful gifting of God.

Only persons are *whole* (complete) beings. Subpersonal beings (from molecules to monkeys) are *part* (incomplete) beings. They cannot receive

Facing the Dark Side of Genesis

themselves within themselves and so are not, and *cannot be*, *fully* what they are. (See *excidents*.)

To *be* is to be *unique* (to be not the same as anything else) *and* to be *uniquely related* (to every other being that is). For person-beings, to *be* is (also) to *be-with*.

Existence is a *way* of being, of standing outside of self and other things. *Ex-sistere* means to "stand out of." But God and all created persons who said fully *yes* to creation *ex nihilo* do not *exist*; they simply *are*. They have no passivity to "overcome" by striving to get out of or beyond their condition of being.

All material beings, as we know them now, not only *are*, but *ex-ist*. Subpersonal beings exist by having "parts outside of parts," by being extended, material realities. Personal beings who, like us, have fallen—who are defective—*ex-ist* also by reflective consciousness, whereby they "stand outside" themselves by being conscious of themselves, the better to direct themselves and make choices (the existentialist aspect).

Failure to distinguish meaningfully between *being* and *existence* (in any language equivalent) can be seen as a particularly instructive sign of our originative repression of our *first* act of *be*-ing and of the ex-istence that this act caused.

The *pre-conceptive latency of our fallen being* (*ontological latency*) is the coma-like, disordered way of being from which we emerge at conception. It was caused immediately by the crash of saying *maybe* at the moment of creation *ex nihilo*.

This condition of collapsed being before existence (conception) has nothing to do with reincarnation or even incarnation. There was no "taking on" of any kind. The perfect (finite) ontological structure with which we were gifted at creation *ex nihilo* was compromised by our imperfect response. Immediately, we became imperfect created persons by way of *adding* an *imperfect receiving* to our originative perfection or giftedness. We became, as it were, "bloated in our being." Our perfect, God-gifted essence remained, but our nature—the disposition to act according to essence—was self-distorted.

Maybe-sayers thus subsist prior to their space-time ex-istence at conception. Our pre-conceptive latency is the condition of our being following the moment of *our imperfect response* to originative creation right up to the moment of conception. Our self-conflicted be-ing (including powers to know and love) was relatively dysfunctional until that event. We were not fallen angels, but simply fallen humans.

Energy is the natural capacity to do work: to struggle, strain, move forward, exercise potencies to do and to be done to. It arises from the fractuation (fractured actuation) done by the *maybe*-saying of originatively

Glossary

sinning persons and it comes in many forms at various levels of redemptive causality. Without any originative sin, there would be no need or occasion for energy. Every reality would be a *pure act* or *actuality*—whether infinite or finite. No work to be done. Simply, the play of everlasting life.

Essence is *what* someone or something *is*. While one can focus on the essences of qualities and activities of entities, the prime signification relates to the *fundamental what*: *what* is a person, *what* is this thing or that thing as such. Fundamentally, what *kind* of person or thing is this as different from other kinds of reality?

But there are really two different—almost always confused—kinds of essence: *common* (e.g., human) and *individual* (e.g., *this* human). The confusion between, say, the humanness and Jamesness of James makes for much metaphysical mischief in giving an account of being *as being*. *What James is* as this unique human (his uniqueness of person) is not at all the same as his being a human kind of being.

Nature is the essence of someone or something as this essence is disposed to act. What kinds of activity can we expect from this or that entity? Granted the essence of a peach tree is to produce peaches—not apples, oranges, *et al.*—its nature is the inexorable disposition to do just that. The way the being expresses itself, or can express itself, in action is its nature. *Nature* is, so to say, *how* the *essence* can reveal itself in acting. In saying *maybe* to being and God, the *self acts through* its essence, but *in and by* its nature.

Form (substantial form), traditionally conceived, is that principle in the essence of a person or thing *by which* the entity is *fundamentally what* it is. It is an intrinsic *part* of the essence. All things have substantial forms: one for each kind of thing.

This traditional meaning is considerably modified by the theses of this book. In the new view, substantial form is the principle of the person (not of things) *by which* he or she is able to give self to self and to all others as a principle of essence. In the new view, it is called "givity": the capacity specifically to give in a receiving way. It is the principle that is co-active with matter and is a dimension of the *act* of *be*-ing. To be is to be giftive (and to be receptive).

In the new view, human *souls* are the substantial forms *as they serve* human persons in their recovering from defective exercise of "givity" at the moment of their originative creation. Souls as (reparative) substantial

Facing the Dark Side of Genesis

forms serve fallen humans in their struggle to attain the pristine, God-intended condition of gifting selves fully at the moment of creation.

Matter (prime matter), traditionally conceived, is that principle in the essence of a human person or thing *out of which* the entity is *fundamentally what* it is. Matter is an intrinsic part of the essence. All things in matter and motion, space and time, involve prime matter, from which every diverse kind of thing is developed. It is the ultimately common feature of substances in the cosmos. None can exist without it. This traditional meaning is, however, considerably modified—not negated—by the theses of this book.

Prime matter (reconceived in the light of Faith and ontological reflection), first of all, is the principle of the human *person* (not of any *thing*) *by which* he or she is able to receive self from within self as a characteristic of essence. (Angels have no prime matter. Their kind of essence itself is pure receptivity to their be-ing.) (God's Being is pure *infinite* receptivity, as well as infinite givity.) This pure receptivity-power, co-constitutive of the essence, was gifted at the moment of creation *ex nihilo*.

In the new view, matter is a kind of *receptivity*: the capacity to *receive* one's essence in a giving way—and not at all "to be done to" or "to be determined." The prime matter and substantial form are totally correlative as the roots of all receiving and giving in the human person from the moment of originative creation.

Originative matter was *purely* **active receptivity**—*the active power or potency to receive who and what* we are. It was not—originatively—the *passivity* or passive receptivity delineated by Aristotle.

Pure originative receiving is just as active and real as giving. *Originatively*, there is no passivity.

With our bad originative response, prime matter as sheer receptivity within our essence had to begin functioning as prime matter that is passive, a capacity to "be done to" right within the essence and to function in common with the extrinsic energy of subpersonal creation. Out of this passive condition, human bodies were formed. Our bodies are prime matter *as it serves* human persons in attempting to attain the pristine condition of receptivity intended by God at the moment of creation.

Angelic persons, however, in their greater simplicity and likeness to God's infinite receptivity, are without this co-principle within their essence. Originatively, angels are simple, sheer receptivities for the act of be-ing.

Glossary

The following terms—except purely active potency—apply strictly to existents in the cosmos, not to angelic creatures.

Substance is, above all, quite like what Aristotle said it was in the first instance (primary substance): this whole being...its essence, with all its attributes and weaknesses, concretely and singly. More specifically, in accord with the common tradition, substance (second substance) is also that principle in the being of a person or thing *by which* the entity is or exists *in and through itself* and not in and through any other. Every created substance is its own principle of intrinsic being and activity (but not its own ultimate cause). It remains the source of natural stability in the midst of accident-modifications or changes. In space and time, substance relates to accidents as passive potency (*q.v.*), out of which qualities and acts develop.

Accidents are not the substance, but parts of the substance, through which the substance *manifests itself*. An accident, such as the color of a tree or the thought of a human, does not be or exist in and through itself, but only *in and through another* (a substance). The act of walking and even the power to walk, as instances, are accidents and cannot be or exist "on their own" or in and through themselves. There is no act of walking without a walker, nor act of thinking without a thinker. Yet the acts are real; they express or manifest the substance or agent and are never to be discounted—even if minor.

Excidents, according to the new view, are the super-multiplicity of substances and their accidents in the cosmos that are not *entitatively* human. Excidents are *everything in the whole of space and time*, including every particle of organic and inorganic matter—and excluding human substance (persons) with all their accidents. At the base of all excidents lies a supremely low level of human (non-entitative) fallen freedom empowering the telic character of all matter and motion. All material things tend, however erratically, to an end or fulfillment of inherent purpose by virtue of their being entities created by God out of fallen human freedom (energy).

At the moment of creation *ex nihilo*, *excidents* resulted from the ontological explosion caused by our immediate response. They are forms of the passive-reactivity (i.e., energy) emanating from the originative sin that was constituted by the first acts of innumerable humans who said *maybe* to be-ing. These elements of discarded human freedom were separated from the malreceptive, freedom-abusive sinning persons

Facing the Dark Side of Genesis

themselves. As subpersonal (partial) beings (molecules to monkeys), they were developed by God's *infinitely* loving activity of compassion on the *maybe*-sayers.

Energy originally emanated from the primal partial rejection (the fractuality) of the perfect personal beings that we were gifted to be. All energy is originatively human energy—frustrated human freedom—and is of two basic kinds: *fragmental* and *non-fragmental*. On the one hand, excidents are *fragmental* energy, "broken off" from the substance of the *maybe*-sayers in the ontological "big bang." On the other hand, fallen human substances retained a kind of *non-fragmental* energy that is therapeutic and intrinsic to them. The result is our defective substances with their accidents (including bodily life in the cosmos).

Active potency is the ability or capacity to *do* something or to *perform* a certain kind of activity. By creation *ex nihilo* we were gifted to *be* pure active potencies of be-ing—each person fully able both to receive and to give personal be-ing. After originative sin, fallen human being has the active (natural) capacity (whether functional or not) to reason and to love; a dog does not. A dog has the active potency to bark and wag its tail; a human does not. *Pure* active potency, however, is the kind of being we were gifted to be *out of nothing*. It was not mixed with any passive potency. We created the latter by our less-than-full response.

Passive potency is the ability or capacity to *be done to*, to *be affected by* or determined by someone else or something else. A tree has the capacity (passive potency) to be bent by the wind; a boulder does not. A boulder has the capacity (passive potency) to be rolled down a hill; a (living) tree does not.

Moreover, "prime matter" in the traditional sense is a sheerly passive receptivity—prime passive potency. In the new view, however, prime matter is *originatively* a supreme, purely active, receptivity of essence right within the essence—an *active potency*. God does *not*, and cannot, create *directly* out of nothing any passive potency.

As perfectly self-actuated, angels and saints in heaven are purely active potencies that co-act *with* God and the others, without being acted *upon* or determined in any way. There is no *passive* potency in beatitutde.

Glossary

Creation

Creation *ex nihilo* (out of nothing) is the *originative beginning of all finite being*. God infinitely loved persons into being. Only persons resulted—out of nothing, out of no preceding substance. The creation was immediate, non-durational, and immaculate. Each person was unique and perfect in every way, including the freedom (purely active potency) to say *yes* fully. There was no temptation or ability to *be* tempted. Simply, there was gifted an invitation to *being with* God and all others 'ecstatically' forever.

This creation was perfectly *interpersonal* in divine intent and solely an act of God.

Creation *ex aliquo* (out of something) is the (*secondary* or *derivative*) creation of *be-coming*: being coming back to itself from a crash and from its ontological self-conflict. This remedial act of God began at the same moment as creation *ex nihilo* and our response. God "works with and out of" the results of the originative crash of those persons who said *maybe* to the gift of being in the *ex nihilo* creation. Infinite love and power interacts with finite, free resistance that is both conscious and unconscious.

This redemptive opportunity for salvation of these "fallen human persons" is what is directly the subject of the *Book of Genesis* and other Scriptures. According to Christian teaching, this redemptive creation of *becoming* culminated in the death and resurrectional life of Jesus Christ. At least, it can be said that, for all three theistic traditions, only God can redeem and save us.

While originative *creation* is interpersonal, but solely the act of God, *salvation* itself is an interpersonal act of finite freedom completely cooperating with infinite freedom.

Immaculate creation is another name for the interpersonal, immediate, durationless originative creation *ex nihilo* by which God gifted into being perfect persons with perfect freedom (as pure and unique acts of personhood, able to receive their being perfectly). The result of God's act of creating was beings unstained by any passivity at all. All gifted persons (angelic and human) were purely (immaculately) who and what they were by the power of the infinitely loving heart of God and necessarily gave their interpersonal response (*yes*, *no*, or *maybe*).

Facing the Dark Side of Genesis

Freedom and Sin

Freedom is the correlative capacity of intellect and will to let the person be present to, and unite with, the Being of God *and* to participate in the fundamental goods of human personhood. Essence-freedom is structured to unite directly with—*not an identity with*—the essence of God, if or when beatitude is attained.

Natural freedom is, then, the *essential disposition* to know and to love, to the fullest extent of one's capacity of be-ing.

Functional freedom is the actual doing of the knowing and loving. Both natural and functional freedom are gifted in originative creation. But the defective response of our first act of freedom maimed them both, functionally separating them from each other and from the freedom of essence, the being as originatively gifted.

The alternatives of *yes*, *no*, or *maybe* were not set up "ahead of time." Our originative freedom was "pre-alternative." Before we broke out into the alternative conditions of being-and-becoming, we were *free*—like God—only to say *yes*. But being finite, we were *able* to say *no*. We were not *free* to say *no*; but we were *able* and did, *de facto—severely damaging our freedom.* Only then did arise the passively based kind of freedom with its alternatives and choices.

Originative sin is our *first maybe* (less than a full *yes*), said to God and ourselves with perfect, untempted freedom at the non-durational, immediate moment of creation *ex nihilo*. The degree of *no* in that *maybe* is not the only cause, but it is the ultimate cause, of all evil *in which we find ourselves involved*.

This primal sin caused our very exposure to the evils done by others—including the forces of Satan—as well as evils done by ourselves. Without originative sin we would be completely blissful in be-ing. By this abuse of perfect freedom we are now in the cosmic world of space and time—"all spaced out" and "doing time."

Original sin in Eden is a subject for *reportorial* Revelation. It is known by Faith in Scripture and Tradition. *Originative* sin, however, is a subject for our *personal* admission. It was not one of our temporal decisions or events, and thereby could not be readily "reported." But it can be *admitted* in the light of Revelation. This signature sin is received unconsciously by Faith in Scripture and Tradition; and it is discerned, at least somewhat, by awareness of our being as *be*-ing—by beingfully (ontologically) received Faith.

Original sin is the first recorded historical sin. Adam and Eve committed this disobedience as they were tested through the serpent. God "predicted" it in saying that on the day you "eat of it (the forbidden fruit), you will die

Glossary

the death." This sin manifested to Adam and Eve their own weakness already present in the Garden of Eden as the result of their *ontologically* prior and repressed *originative* sin, committed along with all the rest of us. The *original* sin in Eden initiated the execution of the punishment of *originative* sin for all of us. It included our generation in the world of space and time, that made it possible for us to wake up to our sinfulness and our need for a Savior.

Knowing

Knowing is, quintessentially, a personal activity by which we are related intentionally to the being and essence of everyone and everything. It is proper to all persons. Every person is doing it, even if unconsciously. Despite our present degree of consciousness, therefore, knowing is also vastly unconscious for those of us in the fallen world. The largely repressed origin of unconscious knowing is our response in the moment of creation *ex nihilo*.

Starting from our present fixation on an implicit framework of space and time for everything, *we think that* conscious knowing in this world *initiates* the connection between knower and known, between ourselves and the world we are knowing. But the connection or "intactness" is already there—having been buried by our ontological repression.

Knowing in the spatiotemporal world, then, is remedial—a knowing derivative of the primal knowing, done by our being as be-ing. It is the tip of the iceberg.

We cannot not know, in some manner—however remotely and confusedly—all that is. To be is to know (finitely, for created persons) all that is, at least to some degree. God is known by everyone, whether consciously or unconsciously or partly both. So, too, is known everyone in creation, spiritual and temporal (past, present, and future). Unconscious, subconscious, and preconscious knowing are bases, out of which *conscious* knowing occurs.

Sensory knowing is also real, but peripheral, and not necessarily personal (i.e., as in animals). By sensation alone—whether internal or external—the essence of anything is never known.

We have been hardened perennially by the idea that there is nothing in the intellect that was not first in some manner in the senses. So, we instinctively think that substantial knowing is a kind of "gap jumping." By the power of its "intentionality" (other-directedness) and by the light of an "agent intellect," the ordinary (potential) intellect is thought to initiate contact with the essences of people and things (called "objects" of

Facing the Dark Side of Genesis

knowledge) by 'jumping the gap' between knowing power and known realities.

Such a knowing, however, is found only in redemptive creation (*ex aliquo*). This knowing is itself founded on the gapless and super-dynamic radiation of knowledge coming from the ever-nurturing originative knowing at the moment of creation *ex nihilo*. In that originative creation, we knew, *and still know, all that is*, by our *finite* powers of intellect and will, now so sorely abused. The common practice of identifying knowing as *solely within* our earthly predicament reinforces our originative repression and keeps us "locked out" of the depths of our be-ing and a much fuller meaning for who we are even at present.

The empirical and quasi-empirical dimensions of intellection here and now beg for support from the strictly non-empirical, but archetypally relevant dimensions. Wisdom is a loving kind of knowing and a knowing kind of love.

Conscious is the manner of knowing that we all desire now. As experienced in the present world, conscious knowing is necessarily narrow, focused, and precludes much. Nevertheless, before we know things consciously, we know them unconsciously, perhaps also subconsciously, definitely preconsciously, and above all, protoconsciously. Conscious knowledge and awareness of someone or something can come about in various ways (such as immediate intellection or intuition, instruction from another, recalling or memory, individual or collective probing and investigation, meditation, contemplation, and so forth).

Subconscious is the manner of knowing things that are just below the surface of consciousness. We are always knowing subconsciously particular things, many of which are semi-conscious, or at least partially conscious. Subconscious things often can be readily brought to consciousness. How to do ordinary tasks such as eating, washing dishes, playing tennis, playing the piano, and all manner of "automatic" activities constitute one major area of the subconscious.

Unconscious is the repressed manner of knowing persons, things, and meanings that are buried deeply away from conscious life. Much is rarely accessible to consciousness as formed in this world. But the whole of the unconscious plays its part in influencing thought and behavior. It is meaningful to distinguish the emotional or psychic unconscious (recognized psychoanalytically) from the spiritual and ontological unconscious, so prominent in this book.

We might even speak of the physical unconscious. It includes all human physiological and physical actions of which we are not conscious. Together, the physical, the psychic, and the spiritual unconscious—

Glossary

including the "collective and archetypal unconscious"—form a virtually horizonless ocean of potential meaning.

Some have represented the unconscious as featuring levels. Included are the subconscious, along with various kinds of deeply buried meaning.

From the ontological standpoint in this book, we know *protoconsciously* everything that is. Such knowledge was "smashed and packed down" by the sin forming our *unconsciousness*. Therefore, when we consciously know something in this world, especially new meanings, we do not simply come to know it "out of the blue." Rather, we come to *know that we know* it finitely, and with much inadequacy.

Preconscious (non-Freudian) is the manner of knowing persons and activities that are *spiritually unconscious*. Persons and activities that are critical to our being are particularly known in this way. The preconscious area of reality occurs prior to the development of ordinary consciousness. It is most directly beingful in its bearing upon us. This ontological level of knowing—in this book, the spiritually unconscious—is quite closely associated with our originative act of freedom in creation *ex nihilo*.

Protoconscious is the manner of knowing by which we originatively received our be-ing from God. It is our originative knowing of God, self, and all others at the non-durational, first moment of creation. This is the archetype of what we now know and call consciousness: our ordinary consciousness that is partial, functional, and privileged as redemptive.

Repression is the unconscious denial that we know some event, actuality, emotion, feeling, or value even as we *do know it unconsciously*. This mechanism of human knowing is an attempt to protect the knower from impulses, images, concepts, memories, meanings, and values that would likely cause anxiety and various disturbances. Repression is never good, but often inevitable.

The supreme instance of such "protection" is our immediate denial to ourselves of what we failed to do at the moment of being created out of nothing. This prime repression keeps us from recognizing our originative sin, the ultimate cause of *all* evil in our lives. It virtually requires blaming Adam, Eve, the serpent, and God for originating our predicament.

Psychoanalytic repression—repression of unwanted emotional and mental content—is better known at present and to be taken seriously; but it does not even get near to the root of our spiritual denial of originative sin. The latter is the supreme reason for all repression and suppression.

Facing the Dark Side of Genesis

Suppression is the *conscious* attempt to be unaware of, or not to attend to, the multiplicity of events, actualities, emotions, feelings, or values that flood our everyday lives. Generally, it is a good and necessary endeavor that is ongoing and allows us to concentrate on one thing at a time. Often it is an explicitly deliberate attempt to block awareness of something undesirable. This activity can be good or bad, depending on the issue at hand.

Suppression is a conscious activity, even if quick and minimally explicit. Repression, however, is always an unconscious activity.

Intellect

In the new view, intellect and will are co-dimensions of the *be-ing* that each created person *is*. They are the "know and love" powers of *be-ing*. To be, for a person, is to *know* and to *will*. It is impossible for a person to *be* without also knowing and willing *protoconsciously*—however well or poorly.

Intellect and will are more than simply faculties of reparative and recuperative action in the world of be-coming, as we first come to be aware of them. They *are* the created being as knowing and willing (loving or hating) originatively and forever.

Potential Intellect is the power to know *by which* we are in touch with, and called to become wedded to, the essence and being of everyone and everything good.

In our common earthly life, this power does the conceiving, judging, and reasoning. It operates in being determined ("stimulated") by the objects of knowledge. It is the ability to be-done-to by whatever it conceives. It is ecstatically fulfilled in heaven, and is an instrument of supreme self-torture in hell.

Agent intellect, in traditional thought from Aristotle onward, is a pure act of intelligibility-giving. It is characterized as a supreme light that renders what is potentially knowable by the potential intellect actually knowable. It is a supreme instrument of knowledge, without itself being a knowing power.

In the new view, however, agent intellect is the originative capacity to *know* (fully and directly)(a purely active power to know)—to be united with all persons, infinite and finite, in their being and essence. It is the only way *knowing* transpires in heaven.

Glossary

Will

Potential Will is the power, in space and time, to love *by which* we affirm, and are called to unite with, the essence and being of everyone and everything good. The objects of the will determine or "act upon" it in the holistic processes such as loving, desiring, delighting, being repelled, and the like. Thus will functions in the redemptive creation as a critical means of coming to what God has prepared for those who would love forever.

Agent Will is the power to love, to say *fully yes* to God, self, and others immediately and forever—right from the originative beginning. From "moment one" in creation, we did not fully exercise it. This power is now almost totally repressed.

In classical philosophy, the missing elements are curious concerning the agent (active) intellect and the agent (active) will. The agent intellect is portrayed as not knowing anything. And the notion of an agent will is virtually non-existent. But one cannot reasonably conceive of intellect without a corresponding will, and *vice versa*. That idea has been axiomatic in terms of the traditional understanding of potential intellect and potential will. Such can be no less true for active intellect and active will.

It is interesting to realize that the classical tradition recognizes, from the thought of Aristotle, the reality of an agent (purely active) *intellect*. But it fails to acknowledge it as *both* a light *and* a purely receptive knowing power for executing a pure act of knowing.

Nowhere, however, do we find acknowledgement of a truly agent (purely active) *will* by which we committed our personal originative sin, but could have instead related perfectly with God forever.

At the heart of all knowing and loving, **agent intellect** is our purely active power of emphatically receiving ourselves and others, even as **agent will** is our purely active power of emphatically *gifting* to ourselves and others. In hell, **agent will** represses itself so severely that one can blame all adversity on God. In heaven, **agent will** is our central loving power, uniting us with God in utter bliss forever.

By their originatively defective activity, agent intellect and agent will are found in this world to have been largely passivized (contaminated). Yet every passive condition of intellection and of volition requires, as its base, a purely active agency, as gifted by God at the core of one's being. Only by agent will, for instance, can we love God with our "whole mind and heart." The slightest passivity prevents wholeness of activity.

Facing the Dark Side of Genesis

Loving

Loving is willing the truest and best for self and *all* others, despite the cost. Not wanting or wishing, but *willing*. Our loving comes in degrees of intensity. At any given time, however, we love everyone, including God, with the same intensity. Often confused with liking, loving has nothing *essentially* to do with pleasure and pain. Love of enemies and of friends is the call to all that they may live well the be-ing with which they were originatively gifted.

At any given moment, we love everyone with the same *intensity*, but we know and love some persons with much greater *richness* than with others, based on our mutual experience, affection, and value sharing. If we were to consider whom we *love* least in this world: we can know that *that* is how *intensely* we love God, all others, and ourselves.

Affirmational love (see *loving*) is the central form of at least five kinds of love. Affirmation is the attitude of spontaneously delighting in another person and giving the other to himself or herself in an unqualified manner. The beloved feels loved and gifted as good unconditionally by the lover. Obviously, God is the supreme Gifter of being: of gifting to another (the created person) his or her whole being, without any "strings" attached.

Traditionally, *storge, eros, philia,* and *agape* are often cited. In general, they are forms either of giving others to self (such as *eros*) or of giving self to others (such as *agape*).

None of these, however, expresses the central meaning of love found in *originative creation*. And when created persons come to realize *existentially* how they have been gifted by God, they are much better able to "pass it on" in attitude and in deed to their companions in being. God's act of creating was an *infinite willing* of each of us to *be*, to be this unique person, and to *be-with* God—literally giving us to ourselves to *be* forever.

Friendship is a relationship that is of genuine love (see above) in which the persons share some sense of equality and esteem, including affection, and an ever-increasing participation in common values. The depth of the friendship can be assessed by the degree to which the friends participate in the most fundamental, spiritual values of human life. We *love* our friends more richly than others, but not more intensely.

In brief, friendship is loving plus liking. It is opposite to "enemyship," that is, loving plus disliking.

Glossary

Assorted Terms

Experience is the conscious participation in the world of space and time. It is essentially a *felt being-done-to*. It can be pleasant or unpleasant, happy or unhappy, by virtue of how one's consciousness is affected by the interaction with others and the movements of the self.

Experience is a bit like the wrapping or insulation on an electric wire. It can serve as a protection from what is really going on, what is going through the wire. Or it can be stripped away…by death. Experience is the conscious impact upon us of the world of passive potency.

But our activities or acts that the experience surrounds are independent of the "wrapping" or experience. We inveterately fail to identify the difference between acting and being acted upon while acting, even as we fail to identify the difference between being and existence. Ex-perience happens only in ex-istence and in our outsideness kind of agency. Every experience—including the mystical—"hides" an act or acting that is at least a little bit other than the experience itself, even as every existent—being that ex-ists—hides the act that is the be-ing of it all….However positive our experience is, it is basically passive (passive-reactive in the ontological sense).

There is no experience in heaven. No beatific *experience*. Just sheerly ecstatic, egoless participation in the Being of God and of one another—incomparably more joyful than any *experience*. The heart of acting and co-acting is passivity-free, existence-free, and experience-free. All is be-ing and lov-ing in consummate joy.

Experience provides opportunity for learning here in creation *ex aliquo*. But experience is not "the best teacher." It is not a teacher at all. The one who experiences teaches self or is taught *through* experience, not *by* it.

Perfection is a term that literally suggests the fulfillment of a process, a making (*per-facere*, to make through and through). Nevertheless, traditionally, it seems to be purged of any suggestion of process as when it is applied to God and angels. For the most part, it means *flawless, without blemish or defect*.

The scholastic philosophers and theologians made much of a distinction between what they called pure and mixed perfections. Pure perfections are those attributes such as intellect, knowledge, love, truth, *et al.* that do not necessarily suggest any passivity or "limitation." Mixed perfections are those qualities that necessarily are a mix of actuality and passive potency, such as colors, sounds, bodies, *et al.*

In the new view, these perspectives on perfection are included, but a new and critical emphasis is placed on the difference between perfection (flawlessness) that is *finite*, including the immediate *effects* of the divine Creator's action, and perfection that is *infinite* (God).

Created goodness, for instance, is not fulfilled in infinite Goodness, but in its own kind of *finite* gifted *perfection*.

We are fulfilled *by* God—and by our cooperative selves. But God is not (pantheistically) our fullness. This fullness is finitely perfect, not infinitely perfect. Infinite goodness is the only ultimate *cause* of our complete fulfillment, but not the fulfillment of our perfection itself.

Conception (human) is our individual entry into the cosmos. Prior to conception we were redeemable, but we were almost entirely dysfunctional. Conception is not the beginning of the person's *being*, but the *beginning* of the *becoming* (positive growth and awareness)—the person's coming back, within God's redeeming action, to a condition of originatively-intended *being*. Conception *happens to* the person and initiates formal participation in the spatiotemporal dimension of redemptive activity.

Death is the exit of a redeemed person from the opportunities of the awakening, alerting life in the cosmos. It is entry into everlasting destiny, through divine judgment—into heaven, hell, or final purgation for heaven. What is left in space and time are the *remains* of that person's cosmic participation. The corpse is not the body itself, but "exhaust" from the person's dynamic thrust through space and time.

The internal or spiritual body by which the earthly participation was specifically effected goes with the person and is not separated from the soul. What is separated is the person's empirical (placenta-like) connectedness with life in cosmic matter.

The soul and ontological body are reparative dimensions of the originative form (givity) and matter (receptivity) of the person. They could not separate from each other, without loss of *essential ontological integrity*. In hell, they are "impossibly united" as essential parts and are inexorably at war with each other forever. In heaven, they are "radiantly harmonious" with each other forever.

Grace is the infinitely affirming Being of God as gifting us with the union of love and perfect friendship. The grace of creation—being brought to be "out of nothing" in an unlimitedly unconditional way—is the supreme gift that we failed to receive *fully*. The grace of redemption and of salvation is the same open union of love offered to us in myriad ways throughout our lives and correlates with the grace of sanctification.

Reading Available from *LifeCom* in the **Two Creations Series**

Affirming Our Freedom in God:
The Untold Story of Creation
(LifeCom, 2001) 100 pages

The Cry of Why, beneath the Holocaust; Are We Hiding Something? God Freely Creates Our Freedom to Create, *et al.*

Facing the Dark Side of Genesis:
A New Understanding of Ourselves
(LifeCom, 2008) 84 pages, including Glossary

The Genesis Gap; Originative Sin; Theology of the Person's Being; Two Creations: Originative and Redemptive; Consequences for a Life of Faith, *et al.*

A Perfect Creation:
The Light behind the Dark Side of Genesis
(LifeCom, 2008) 170 pages, including Glossary

From Chaos to Cosmos; The Missing Infinity of God; God's Intimate Act of Creation; The Meaning of Evil and Its Cause, *et al.*

The following comprehensive volume may be pre-ordered:

When God Said Be, We Said Maybe:
An Inside Story of the Creation, the Crash, and the Recovery
(LifeCom, 2009) 480 pages, including Glossary

Booklets:

The Origin of Pain and Evil
(LifeCom, 2008) 35 pages

The Immaculate Conception: An Inside Story
(LifeCom, 2008) 20 pages

LifeCom
Box 1832, St. Cloud, MN 56302
www.Lifemeaning.com

www.ingramcontent.com/pod-product-compliance
Lightning Source LLC
Chambersburg PA
CBHW020017050426
42450CB00005B/507